Thank You, Burnout

From depletion to peace

Hayley Hughes

About the author

Hayley Hughes is an Australian author and working mother who writes to heal. Her debut memoir, *Thank You, Burnout*, is a journal *through* burnout to newfound life. Hayley's writing offers a sincere example of finding peace in a world so complicated and burnt out.

Rich in poetic portrayals of courage, vulnerability, healing, self-help and personal transformation, Hayley's story aims to inspire hope in others facing self-imposed overwork and unsustainable ambition.

Hayley holds a Bachelor of Communication (Business) and has been the recipient of academic and corporate excellence recognition throughout her career.

In 2024, burnout compelled Hayley to trade her successful general practice management career for a more fulfilling life. Prior to her fifteen-year contribution to primary healthcare management, Hayley also excelled within the corporate sector across communications and sales roles.

Today, Hayley works at a specialist practice.

Home for Hayley and her family is a small acreage block on the edge of the forest in Queensland, Australia. Hayley's husband, two sons and two Australian kelpies share her fondness for their green sanctuary, hidden creek and all.

Copyright © Hayley Hughes 2026
First published by Hembury Books in 2026
hemburybooks.com.au
info@hemburybooks.com

Paperback ISBN 9781923517240
Ebook ISBN 9781923517233

hayleyhughes.au

A catalogue record for this book is available from the National Library of Australia

Disclaimer
Please always consult a qualified medical professional for the management of your health and wellbeing. No ideas, words, phrases or concepts throughout offer or serve as medical or life advice. The author is not a medical professional or authority of any sort, and this book is not intended as a substitute for diagnosis or treatment. This book contains descriptions of sensitive topics related to mental distress. These topics may be triggering or distressing for some readers. If you or someone you know is experiencing mental health difficulties, please seek medical support.

For Jackson and Leo, my beautiful boys. I love you.
Family is the most important thing.

Contents

Preface

Burnout is a self-inflicted punch in the face. The victim is also the aggressor in this twisted feud.

Punching yourself in the face is easier than it sounds. Wrong, but doable when people-pleasing graces your DNA. Each irrational strike breaks something inside, packing a lingering emotional sting. Tender, invisible bruises mark the pain of the pieces of yourself given and eroded.

Accepting the abuse and entering the ring for more is never part of the plan. But the martyr within you absorbs the blows, stranded and unsure of how to escape, while your inner offender prepares for ongoing exploitation. *More is fine, thanks for the opportunity.*

Each round repeats the last, conditioning you to your new environment, unable to tap out.

I battered my soul to a pulp while burnout wiped the floor, hiding the emergency behind yet another *yes*. You see, burnout is a first-world problem caused by the first world. First world logically, geographically and socially, and first world personally and spiritually—the world inside; our own first world.

Healing, too, is both situational and internal. The same exertion that fuels burnout is also a requirement of recovery. A project of equal measure, daunting and large, but directed towards the most vital bottom line—yours. The difference is the outcome, the result—a freedom distinct from your familiar prison of exhaustion.

How is your balance sheet? How healthy is your business and busyness of self? burnout asks, prods, shouts. Burnout occurs despite good deeds, often the product of overabundant acts of service with little regard for self. As we add more, our shiny first world celebrates and praises our success. We do too. Burnout creeps and we fade, burying ourselves deeper in the lie of *fine*.

If you're questioning whether you are burnt out, chances are, you are. I hope my story serves as an example. These conversations with self record my journey *through* burnout to somewhere far better. In the year I navigated breakdown, I also experienced some of the best times of my life. If this is possible, anything is.

For once, I had no agenda. Instead, I wrote because I was without-a-hope lost. I wrote to document real and aspirational growth, to mark progress and missteps, to process and stay accountable to myself. I didn't compose my journals for sharing and had no intention of compiling a book. But if I'm honest, writing rescued my life, and so I hope that releasing this might offer encouragement to someone else. We are here to help each other, to relate, to find our way again, and my journal entries share how I found more than expected *thanks* to burnout. Odd, I know.

Earning success while yearning for relief was tough. Burnout struck with a swift hand but it built up with unassuming steadiness. My story's familiar: young family, ambitions, stressful career and side projects all occurring simultaneously. Had I begun writing when burnout first appeared, my entries would date back a long way. Sad to say, I didn't awaken to this until 2024. It's ironic, but breakdown was a powerful call.

The illusion of coping looks different for each of us, and I was a pretty skilled illusionist: graceful and in control while self-destructing, one sleepless night after another. My mind wouldn't stop. My to-do lists were unsustainable, and I worshipped a workload that was eating me alive. I strived on anyway until my new moderator, burnout, burnt me out.

Early full disclosure: my writings don't define burnout in a formal sense because there's much literature on this topic deserving of attention and others that feed into recovery. Awareness is increasing because burnout is affecting more of us more than ever. Trends aside, I do not intend to provide advice, research or a recipe for healing, and I'm unable to promise outcomes. Only we can do that for ourselves. I share to provide relatability and evidence of genuine happiness on the other side of change with the hope that someone, somewhere, might say *me too*. There's comfort in that, enough for me to expose my private vulnerabilities. What was possible for me may also be possible for you.

These are my words, raw and honest, because if you're navigating burnout, I suspect you're seeking a look into a real and nerve-deep, lived experience. Real life doesn't fit into the tidy structure we imagine, and burnout is part of real life. This book honours the roughness of it all to enhance the benefit to you, the reader. Every day I sat to write, I healed a little more. If my story transfers even the tiniest aspect of hope, I've won once again.

Before we go on, it's imperative to note that nothing about my external life is grand or bad. I'm a nobody who found peace and place on my own terms, blessed with my healthy children, Jackson and Leo, love from all directions, opportunity and means. But there's an internal world available that I only recently found.

It is northern lights-level beautiful, with no end to possibility. I hope you too stumble, leap, walk or run towards these expansive fields of wildflowers now or when you need to. Everything will feel uncertain at first, but you'll know when you arrive.

If anything, trust that there's light. Trust that breakdown can be the catalyst for newfound life. I didn't envisage being thankful for such a dark experience, but here I am. My journey through burnout, as you'll discover, more than justifies the unexpected thanks. And if you're sceptical about the thanking burnout premise, I understand. It's a strange take, but gratitude serves. I'll show you.

Ahead of entering my journal, I'll say that my burnout *achievement* went something like this...

Situations and contributors amplified my burnout over time, but the responsible party was *me*. My perfectionistic expectation that all I do must be my best by far aligned me for turmoil, but also transformation. Talk about self-made! I'm certain "do-it-yourself burnout" didn't feature in any curriculum I considered, but I found it, selected this beast of a life elective and fleshed it out into an MBA of personalised pain.

However, to be clear, nobody asked me to work the way I did. That too is on my tab, completely my treat. Ineffective at declining requests, I operated beyond capacity for years. My list of continuous achievements is as lengthy as my long flowing hair. Tertiary scholarships, accolades, promotions, praise, offers of more responsibility; I was in positive, forward and upward motion, all the time. For a while, this confirmed that I was ascending a worthy summit. Wrong.

Throughout my career in general practice management, I contributed to and in time oversaw various aspects of a complex healthcare business for years as part of a senior team and later alone. I adored my role and learning from generous mentors. Pushing beyond limits is how I excelled. Fast-moving stress came with the job, although managing a primary care facility through a pandemic redefined frontline, pivot and pressure. A tale for another book.

Anyway, in 2023 and 2024, my responsibilities expanded to include a key facilitator role in the practice and property's sale following decades of unchanged ownership while maintaining the day to day.

With excitement, I accepted this next opportunity and completed the months of additional work behind the scenes, solidifying my reputation for getting things done.

True to form and with delight, I stored the cards and messages of thanks amongst my prized possessions, oblivious that they held the clues to why burnout knocked me further than a home run.

Your incredible efforts getting the sale over the line were superhuman and exceptional. —Past practice director.

You do a wonderful job of making the most difficult tasks seem manageable, and that is a rare trait. Thank you! —Mentor and predecessor.

Thank you for your empathetic and ethical leadership style. I have no idea how you display such grace under pressure. You are always busy but have time for everyone. Your guidance, encouragement, enthusiasm, thoughtfulness and kindness are unparalleled. You inspire me every day here to be my best. It is abundantly clear how much you put into this job and its employees. It is hard but you make it look easy. —Teammates.

My body faltered as I worked to assist the new practice owners. I ignored my increasing anxiety, weight loss, trembling hands, racing heart, worry, fog, emotional lows, overwhelm and insomnia for a little while. I'd be okay soon, I told myself, so I kept moving fast.

As expected, the ownership transition came with challenges, but I aspired to be helpful and wanted to stay, so I agreed to please more people, no matter the cost. I was the go-to person on the ground who descended to literally that.

This all compounded my career-long stint of arriving home as my children climbed into bed. I missed family dinners more times than I prefer to admit, and when I did clock off, I was forever fielding a stream of work nonsense in my personal hours. Compassion fatigue can be a legitimate enemy to an empath!

At one point, I correlated the number of times I emailed myself reminders and tasks in the early hours of the morning as an indicator of how far I was falling. Things weren't improving. Exhaustion cocooned me, alongside guilt that the kids would both hit double digits soon and I had already missed so much.

In truth, I lacked the time and capacity to do *everything* to the high standards I set. The situation had to improve, but change was one more thing to add to my list. I had many lists. Long ones.

While building our careers, my husband, Steven, and I embraced continual real estate projects spanning twenty years, including a challenging one-to-two-block land subdivision and intact home removal.

Watching our home drive away on the trays of two Mack Trucks, we were sure that project, which Covid forced us to abandon ahead of the ambitious rebuild stage (also another book), would be our largest, but it wasn't. It would be one of many in the timeline of our lives.

Just as the two-year subdivision headache was winding down and before burnout came to say hello during the practice sale, my brother and I unexpectedly inherited a farm—one side of a mountain, to be exact, in the nearby hinterland. More on this coming up. The point is, we were doing it, succeeding, sometimes failing, and so grateful for the support from our families. Our efforts returned steady rewards, but the hectic pace and weight escalated. By choice, I ran my life as an ultra-marathon without pit stops at sprinting speed carrying a weighted backpack. Not normal. My existence morphed into an overwhelming, multitasking mess ruled by personal benchmarks I perceived as correct. I kept volunteering for more, to eternity and beyond. Change was on me, but I did what any high achiever would do: I pressed on until I had nothing left.

"You're *burnt out*, lovie. You need a break." This came from Dad, the experienced, calm and collected calibre of doctor who seldom signals alarm unless there's a genuine concern. His words registered. Time to take notice of the many hints I long denied.

When he said it, looking me in the eye, his hand on mine, the pressure released, melting me to a puddle of surrender. *Burnt out* resonated. My bones gave way, along with my mascara, as I slumped in my seat—and I don't slump.

"Burnout? No. I just have a lot on my plate." For a moment I had a go at upholding my usual *I'm fine* approach, knowing full well I'd long ago reached my limit and would either have to resign or find another solution soon. I knew this well before my chat with Dad.

Hugging me close while I sank further into the chair, Dad didn't suggest what I should do, and I didn't ask. I'd figure things out for myself. I had to. It was the most important part.

To be perfectionist-level sure, I digested all I could about the symptoms of my predicament. Confirmation after confirmation came; I featured in each description on every "About burnout" webpage. I had *achieved* severe burnout. This explained a lot. A strange relief washed over me as I asked myself, *Does this mean I get to stop?*

Prior to my lightbulbs of truth and Dad's gentle wisdom, I hadn't made time to think about burnout, or whatever I thought the experience was. I assumed that keeping my cracked lips above the waterline, gasping for air while embodying *go, go, go; busy, busy, busy* until it hurt, was a reasonable way to live. Denial sufficed for so long.

It's fortunate that context and time—those subtle links between unfolding events, regardless of immediate comprehension—reveal a lot. One day, making sense. Paths wind, twist and deviate, nudging our feet to step towards the pulls of what's required and waiting all along.

Nothing's by chance, though amid crisis I was unaware of both that and fate. I kept circling back to pain, taking longer than healthy to grasp this pattern as a warning, not a mistake. My appreciation and acceptance lay dormant and overlooked until something jolted me awake (even though I hadn't slept well for months).

The unforeseen and the misunderstood became my test, my chance, part of my tale and the most rewarding classroom of my life. Turns out, recognition of burnout, inheriting a farm and writing are my *jolts*, the forces helping me to master peace (one day).

First, the mountain that's played a towering role in my healing: the farm, a spectacular, secluded place that's been in our family since childhood.

It was manned for decades by our late Uncle Robert, who with little notice selected us as the custodians of his mountain, an honour and responsibility of magnitude. A place like no other, it is laden with green in all forms—weeds, flora, diverse rainforests, steep waterfalls and freshwater creeks, but mostly weeds. The farm is home to ancient trees and giant arches of bamboo so vast they touch the sky. As for the dense bush tracks in all directions, we cut our way through, hoping for the best as far as snakes and palm-sized spiders go.

Rough land with walls of green, lush plateaus and grand valley views, away from the busy world, immersed in the wilderness—it's a special property with a complicated backstory and endless potential. For us, for our children, to make something of, our place in wild nature, together.

The eclectic and confronting mix of hoarded rubbish and relics from the past strewn across the 176 acres makes things interesting. Beauty, nature, history and ruin collide here. There are few words to quantify the clean-up that will consume many years ahead. As we sort through, we note any progress as an achievement, a bit like my burnout recovery.

Despite the unique challenge it presents, the farm's not another source of overwhelm. If anything, the timing aligned with precision. The farm is an inviting beginning to an existence greener and higher, providing space, freedom, purpose and meaning. The parallels are poetic. Much of humanity tackles metaphorical mountains through hardship and change. I did too, but many days atop our actual mountain. I doubt I'll encounter more powerful perspective than that offered by the combined forces of burnout and full immersion in nature while healing, but I hope I do.

In some ways, Rob gifted us a project for life, a gesture of love and respect paired with a duty as complex as the mountain itself. The learning, too, is steep. But this is how things go. Extraordinary happenings play out every day, beyond plans made. New possibilities bring chance and challenge, often originating from loss, change or even sorrow while also encouraging renewal. Intimidation and wonder mix well. What comes, if met with an openness to listen, offers growth, even if the only germination that's clear is the rapid-sprouting grass and weeds that appear between weekends riding the mowers and slashers.

The farm, like burnout and writing, found a presence in my story for good reason. Legacy, connection and challenge are only the beginning.

As for the writing, it's a simplistic solution for a far-from-simple situation. Journalling never appealed to me. As in, I was not interested, but writing was my last-ditch attempt to save myself. My first-ever entry on that morning in May 2024 is where this book begins. I wrote in tears; I had nothing else left to try, short of medication or a therapist.

For a while I wanted to write *what's the point*, line after line. My journal wasn't a fix; rather, it was an element of change, a way to offload and become open to something new and uncertain. Soon, those messy pages were my confidant, on call any time. With questions and answers flowing, the words my release, an entry point to another way. On paper, I bolstered a bravery I'd not known, there in black and white. I rationalised and coaxed myself into further change while locating sense in my world and discovering my voice on those pages. Hence, journalling was no longer lame.

Change was upon me, collapse imminent and rest within reach, if I chose well. I didn't know what the future held other than I needed sleep and that it might pay to keep writing. What I can confirm, as you'll see as you read on, is that burnout happened *because* of me and *for* me, forcing a new season, a different life everlasting. You might recognise yourself in these pages. Helpful is my intention.

Part One

Burning and Broken

Morning of 7 May 2024

Desperate and breaking

If I could hold my own hand, I'd guide myself far away with care, so I couldn't find my way back. To a place of escape, where the noise and need no longer grip my neck. I would lead myself home, to my family, to me.

No change, no sleep again, exhausted and running on fumes. My racing mind intensifies as soon as I connect with the pillow. I direct thoughts away, but another comes. Frustrated, anxious, desperate. I must find a lasting solution somehow.

Like clockwork, by 3.45 a.m., I reach for a book to read to induce sleep and disconnect from the intrusive rumination, the gazillion lists and the monster of panic waiting under my bed. My ability to detach or introduce anything that resembles a boundary is slow to progress. Every night, tears flow as I focus my thoughts on the boys instead. With eyes pressed closed, I whisper "Worry serves no purpose" on repeat. But my hopeless murmurs get me nowhere. My growing workload, it's more immense than one person can handle until the end of time and without pause.

It's no wonder day and night have little distinction; the taunting stress doesn't discriminate. Every day I'm awake to hear the morning birds—that distinct species—sing to signal dawn's arrival. Tension wraps me while I listen, as if the tangled sheets are alive, tightly constricting. This routine of lying awake and alarmed night after night tests my resilience and ability to turn struggle into hope. There must be a way, even though my efforts are no match for my reality. Drowning, aching, everything's sore.

Hopefully, a reprieve will come soon; the off button must be within reach. Press it when you can. Even my daily commute to and from the surgery is a challenge to recall, spent firefighting over the phone or holding back desperate tears while speaking with Mum, but the rest is a blur. Mum's offering all she can, yet I'm alone, stunned and lost.

Despite it all, the feedback from my bosses confirms my efforts are notable. My commitment too. The praise is like sunshine, but it's meaningless because "impossible" is an unrealistic expectation. A harmful and sad game for the willing pawn.

Anyway, it's now a week since I resigned then backtracked and agreed to tread water forever when asked to stay, all in the same conversation. What have I done? Why didn't I stick with my decision, the one that required all the courage I have left? When will that clarity come? That's up to me. I'm scribbling this down with one hand and wiping my cheek with the other, regret welling alongside my tears.

I've kept myself stuck, hurting beyond this sharp edge of *enough*. *Enough* is more a culmination than a single event and the only way to describe having nothing left to give. Yet here I am again, in breathless distress at dawn, questioning how I'm going to get through the day. The situation is unlikely to improve.

The answer is still *leave*. But I said I'd try, so I must do that first. Sigh, the generous donor in me won again despite the internal desert of nothingness and my doubt about how I'll sustain.

Today's attempted solutions include:

One coffee instead of two to aid sleep.

Approach the day without concern.

Incorporate breaks. Take a moment. Step away to eat.

Don't forget to breathe. One breath before entering the practice for the day doesn't count.

Revisit protected time to deter the constant interruptions.

Encourage a weekly structure with new owners to lessen the chaotic introduction of unexpected additional responsibility.

Reiterate immediate priorities to narrow focus.

Say no and push back if needed.

Increase delegation attempts.

Stop worrying if everyone's happy.

Remember, I'm human, not a machine.

Find hope within however and whenever you can. You will sort this out.

Evening of 7 May 2024

Longing to turn my brain off

Another day, again larger than the last. Overwhelmed. My head hurts, and I'm unsure of what to think, feel or do. Trust my blaring intuition or explore the meek and mild, no-name flimsy bandaid suggestions for solving this dejected episode of life? If there's anything out there, please give me a sign of some sort.

The enormity and scope of the competing initiatives overfilling my plate feed my ferocious worry. Juggling so much at once while sustaining operations in the wake of the change in ownership is nauseating me. Turns out, covering a couple of combined senior roles with the sale efforts loaded on top is not a smart move. I'm deflated. Yet, I raised my hand to stand under this roaring waterfall without a lifeboat in sight.

Regardless, assisting the front desk team today provided its usual enjoyment. But like everything else, it came at a cost later tonight, when I should have been at home reading a bedtime story with the boys. Instead, I was playing catch-up. I'm attempting to take charge of the demands on me, but unsure if my approach is reliable in this scattered and foggy state. The top priorities live on my desk, a daunting congregation joined by various items that are not priorities at all. There's more and more that requires my attention, creeping out of any small crack, while the incessant and maddening interruption soundtrack blasts off the walls. I can't carry this much longer, but I will continue on.

Situation normal aside, I exposed too much to my new employer. Admitting burnout and asking for help is confronting, but how else to expedite aid where desperately needed? I received immediate kindness and care from good people, thankful for that. Please let actions mirror words.

For now, compress the brakes on my mind to make it through this phase of confused disorder. The throb in my chest booms. What's enduring inside is perishing. The exhaustion's deep, a recurring wound. I'm conscious of hiding the weakness and nervousness in my voice behind each fake smile. My anxiety's visible yet professional, complementary to my smart uniform hanging off me a little more each week.

It doesn't matter what I do; nothing helps. Patience is low as I struggle to stick to my aspirational earlier finish time. My regime of later and later arrivals home lives on. I'm failing the kids, but the photos of them loving their nights with Steven and the caption *Love you, Mum* provides comfort. I miss them.

I'm achieving with all the energy I can muster, although the weight of more is heavy. More keeps coming. I'm far from rested, not as astute as usual and craving space to sort this out. Remove and retreat to thrive again. I wish.

I want out, but I need to try. Stress must reduce, but I'm unable to shut off. Seeking morsels of freedom from the destructive over-whelm is my version of locating the imaginary life jacket that must have come through the mist from that elusive lifeboat near the waterfall. So many questions swirling around. Is it me or the place, the role or the load? Stress is part of the job; this is a huge position. I assume this is typical. If so, why does it feel suffocating and wrong?

Because manageable levels of stress, a reasonable pace, support, options, control over my time, some counterbalance and periods away are all lacking. Thinking about how best to dial down my thoughts is a counterproductive way of breaking my own heart. I can't imagine ever being grateful for or finding reason in this pain. Something has to give or change. My existence is more than work; I have to stop living there. Read, breathe, move, stretch—I'm willing, and will keep embracing it all.

How can I deliver with so few dedicated hours to do *my* work? The minutes in the day are disproportionate to the agendas expected of me, despite logging evenings and weekends. I'm efficient; speed and direction are not the issue. Do I focus on doing what I can and considering it enough, or do I go on neglecting my world to achieve more? For what? I deliver more than most. I'm respected, and I care. This is enough.

I need to get better at putting my thoughts to the side whenever I choose. I get to choose. The option to go remains in my pocket.

I have endless what-ifs around finding a suitable person to assist, and I'm uncertain if assurances will materialise. Let go a little and things will improve. Keep going. It might work. Do the personal work, try as hard there, within. List it out, select what matters today and let the rest wait. Then, brain off until tomorrow.

9 May 2024

Brave face walking a tightrope

The writing helps. Two nights of improved sleep! Grateful I could recoup a little. Refreshed despite fragile is an improvement on broken.

Note to self: keep writing. Expel my conflict onto the page rather than load my recurring dialogue onto someone I love. It's a relief to have an outlet, even if I am a middle-aged weirdo talking to myself. Process via paper so things make more sense. And stop rushing. I'm even racing as I read, write, move, a dominant reflex conditioned to match everything else. Slow down and give to my family and myself first, the way I did yesterday morning.

Relishing that early breakfast with Jackson and Leo made for a pleasant start before walking through the doors of depletion for another big push of a day. I responded with an immediate yes when my boss checked in to see that I was okay. My smile and yes came too fast in my willingness to please. Hand-on-face emoji. Once again, I'm my own saboteur. Typical.

I'm accompanied by an optimistic perspective today. There's something invisible holding me up. Yesterday was a better day if I don't count the late finish. Maybe there's a way. I hope so because efforts to shove my nagging frustrations and the nonstop disruptions aside still resemble an equatorial climate mosquito-swatting mission of shooing the tiny biters away. Stop thinking about it and relax despite the swarm. If I channel laid-back and tranquil, make-believe and pretend might morph into real. Fake-it-till-you-make-it memes may hold some truth.

Voices surround me, talking at me, seagulls chirping as they innocently peck. There are no crispy hot chips in my office to attract them. Fried practice manager is on the menu though, but come in, of course I can help you. Listen and pause before response and action. Find the pressing matters. They are often not the submissions heaped on me from others. Consider the merit of each squawk.

I need to be away from everything. I need to be outdoors. The labour missions at the farm are a step away, a consoling green escape. There's more work than we can point a whipper snipper at and enough scrap metal to launch a recycling plant, but no people. My developing appreciation for the value and appeal of uninhibited places supports the introvert within.

If I Googled my history, the compulsion to succeed, achieve and people-please would top the search. My drive lives on, as does my care for others. I enjoy what I do but can't keep cycling through the repetitive self-torment. My current exertion, in contrast with the tasks at hand, is not constructive; I either lose or eventually pass out. The same outcome. I need to learn to get it done and pack it away. Shrink unnecessary burdens and make room to prosper across other life domains. Don't be shy to say I'm at my limit and time is up for today. Tomorrow offers more of me. Stop sometimes, as foreign as that is.

I'm well aware my ideal stress-versus-rest equation exists to the same degree as a dove-white unicorn. Turn distress into meaningful steps forward, redirect energy and replace this spiral of worry, whatever that looks like. Do the instructions live with the unicorn? Until I find out, revisit favourite books, heed the messages as a plan to cultivate more resilience, if that's even possible. I'm not weak. I'm strong, confirmed by hopeful yet futile attempts to secure a healthier future, untangle my mess, and free my reins. A little solitude mixed with focused achievement is the goal. The occasional solo expedition through the wilderness on a mythical unicorn would be nice too.

11 May 2024

It's the weekend

A good day, despite another draining evening of worry. Hangouts with the boys and some work. A shame, but the emotional tug-of-war is palpable given the quantity. I'm hustling like a loser on the weekend. Why? Don't answer that question. This perpetually awake, looping-through-thoughts approach—it's not working. The anxiety doesn't leave or rest; it's unstoppable. Sleep is key, but despite efforts, I can't find it, an awareness that contributes to my uneasiness and complicit emotional self-harm.

Asleep or awake, I'm scrambling to stop worrying about work when I'm not there. Be kinder to yourself, turn off at home. Repeat the joy with the kids in the backyard this morning. Peaceful and together, I even got some yoga in. Next time, stay still long enough to make it through the relaxing end section of the class. Does sitting amongst the trees for a few moments to gain a little vigour following my eyes-wide-open evening routine of processing the dysfunction count as stillness?

All I know is that each night I sift through the unrealistic, urgent twists and turns and frantic obligations packed and piled on top of the last, as if locked in a congested, noisy subway carriage with no spare overhead handgrips. The destination is without fail two stations forward, five football fields back. The nature of how each mass of additional work lands in my lap immobilises my hope. Everyone needs me for something, as if they join forces to achieve maximum impact (they don't). *Ding, ding, ding.* It doesn't matter what I do. My best preparation is pathetic in comparison to the onslaught of requests. Surrendering to the chaos while bracing tight in a huddled ball might actually be an idea. I'm no match for the puzzling deluge and the constant eleventh-hour asks that blur my focus and progress. There's no chance of touching a project prior to the next one splatting on my keyboard, and my silent rage increases with each call for my help. An uneventful morning or a single boring day would be medicine for my soul.

What do I want? A life. Until I can have it, ask again for someone to lend a hand. My concerns are justified considering the tasks now and ahead. Or do I need to adjust my attitude? I can't handle everything all at once alone. Stop delivering so much to temper the continual and progressive overload because *kind* and *nice* are becoming damaging personality traits. Ensure the word *no* finds a place in my world, fast.

I'm unsure of what else to do now that denial is no longer providing protection from the howling inside. A glimpse of the sunset this evening pacified the scattered, brutal and fractured thoughts that come with burnout, for a moment. There are good days and hard days. Controlled days, and days where the stress erases any headway made. At least there are some good days!

12 May 2024

Questioning everything

A low-key Sunday and a special Mother's Day with my boys. The lost and hyped thoughts continue, but I get a temporary reprieve when I secure these little bites of rest. Sundays are like all other days. My phone's going off with the usual staff stuff, and my anxiety about the mountains of work and the unknown extras that will landslide me tomorrow intensifies the instant I try to disconnect from work. Volume is the problem. It's a vicious cycle that impedes replenishment, a thief of moments, a cruel agitator that pokes. Only I know I'm suffering. Explaining it to others is as effective as asking for help.

And so, I dig my hole deeper as I email myself reminders night and day to repel the thought of each task until I can get to it. It's like shovelling soil onto my head while telling myself I'm launching each heap towards the light above. I imagine it's light, but it could be more incoming work and worry disguised by distance. Covered in dirt, the grit in my eyes induces more tears as the integrity of my mission crumbles in on itself, no matter what I do.

Despite my collapsing emotional pit, I want to live in the moment. How though, when the present is stolen? Nature and family guide me to a better place, but it's not enough. Contemplation has run its course, now as productive and exhausting as the psychological ditch I'm perfecting, the hole that's becoming a trench.

Am I overthinking it? Complete what you can and shut off. Try that again and stop reverting to unhelpful patterns that involve a *yes, no problem, sure, I can do that for you*. Uphold the odd boundary and take a breath after immense effort.

If it's that simple, why is it so difficult to choose my needs? I'm not required to be productive twenty-four hours a day, yet I'm destroying my wellbeing over it. My position description doesn't list "self-destruction of your nervous system", so why am I doing this? Maybe I'm pointing my attention to what's troubling rather than what's worth preserving in some capacity. Whatever the case, my cynicism's tough to shake and contributes to the overwhelm as anxiety's pointless sidekick. Yay for me!

Waning tolerance or not, I must find the good in this next challenging week. I ace challenges; that's where the results are. Is this the issue—that I define failure as giving less than my max? My definitions of success and productivity might benefit from an upgrade. I'm not sure who I am anymore, and I'll require more than a dictionary to locate that characterisation. Or are these emotions part of both crisis and growth, an assorted mix of confusion, exhaustion and pain before I figure it out? Find out.

19 May 2024

Boundaries begin

With sluggish steps, I wandered the uneven forest paths behind home, depleted and adrift. On the track, bordered in arrays of vibrant green, I listened to a podcast on high-achiever burnout. Labels for what I'm experiencing—they're good. The coolness of my morning walk gave way to the warmth from my shower and the sun. Taming anxiety is my aim and an interesting example of willpower's limitations.

Forest walking or otherwise, disbelief lingers following Friday evening's implied pressure to work on into that night and/or over the weekend on *another* new last-minute project as I was packing up for the day well past dark. Without a doubt, unrealistic. Laughable either way, given our recent discussions about burnout, resignation and workloads. It had to be an oversight. On the bright side, I cultivated a win in declining and pointing out the obvious, controlling my fury by an eyelash and leaving for the night. "It's impossible for me to get to this tonight, tomorrow or Sunday," I replied.

I gripped the steering wheel tight the entire trip home, promising myself I wouldn't check emails or engage until Monday. It's now Sunday, and I followed through. I upheld my boundary! I have no guilt about setting limits, only frustration at my situation. Either I let my family down or disappoint others, despite weekends not being part of the arrangement. Alone, it's nothing, an example. Combined, it intensifies the lashing cyclone about to make landfall on my head. This first attempt at courage reveals my general willingness to sacrifice beyond necessary. I set the tone, and that's how senior management goes. I've done my time in spades, so much so I opened the door to burnout, the burnout that penned my resignation letter, the departure I'm placing aside for now. I will prioritise my life this time. There's reassurance in at last opening my arms to self-regard, extending kindness in my direction, not only to those I serve.

In my commitment to self-care, I had to be honest with Steven last night about the dire extent of my distress. The edge of the earth looms close, but he already knew that. He's long prompted me to do what makes me happy, often caring more about my happiness than I do. I share love with a wonderful man. Inscribed across his forehead in invisible ink are the words *Really Great Guy*.

Encased in his bear-hug-worthy arms on the couch before dread, I mean bed, it was the right time to open up. "I don't know what to do," I sobbed. "I don't want to let anyone down. What would you do?"

"But you are letting yourself down," Steven said, pausing the movie. "That's easy—I'd choose myself and my family—but you must do what makes you happy. Everything else will work out."

My next words arrived fast. "I feel like pulling the pin on life would be easier, so I can get some sleep, some relief. It hurts," I confessed. "But I'd never do that. I have too much to lose."

"A job shouldn't make you feel this way. It's just a job! I'll support whatever you choose, but you need some rest. You know your answer."

I nodded. "I'm sorry about all of this; it's a lot on you too."

"It's okay," he said, pulling me close, "but I still hate your job; it's taking so much. Something needs to change."

In a strange way, these wrenching conversations offer welcome solutions and moments of connection in my disconnected state. Remember his words. Help yourself.

While these at-home weekends of both admission and attempted disconnect are helpful, being with my thoughts is confronting. Persistent and deep discomfort stays close. Is this nagging sentiment a message? Instinct teams up with my whole body, screaming at me to walk away. *Take action, sort the rest out later*, it yells. Justifications for and against make it a tricky decision.

Who am I external to my work? I've got the stressed shell of a person down pat. Is there anything else? Tears are ready to spill. Kicking the footy and flying the kite with the boys was this afternoon's effort to remove my opportunity to worry. Taking turns jogging along the grass and sand to launch the kite in low winds did the trick, though the worry will return tonight. My anxiety about going to bed is worse. The mental torture will ramp up again.

Stop damaging myself. This is serious, and the exhaustion enhances my confusion about what I need and how soon I need it. My instincts and the surrounding support will guide me. Also, keep talking with Steven.

20 May 2024

Faking strength to go on

Today was the first day of my bogus attempt at two days' annual leave, where I was needed in the office and took calls. There's no one else to cover logistics; no one as moronic as me. "Attempt" is the key word here. My forced optimism ignored that the weekend gone was subject to pressure and extra work. Or was that a misunderstanding?

Despite being away, I still had one meeting to attend today—an external meeting scheduled way back, so it was best that I went. Of course I went in. Forever available, a sad headline.

Scrolling through my inbox, I dreaded the dump of work I refused to look at late Friday evening in the name of boundaries. The same request was there in writing, reiterating Friday night's flippant verbal download. The substantial left-field and nonessential project would have taken many hours to compile if I could have focused on it without interruptions. Ha ha. Deep breath. I already rejected the unreasonable request, so further explanation is unnecessary.

To add to the comedy, a second email also welcomed me. It arrived Sunday afternoon as the insulting icing on the cake. *Don't worry about the additional items as they were due last week.* Wait, what? I first received the task after 6 p.m. on the date it was due! What if had I toiled away in response to another request on a whim late on a Friday? Unfair and ridiculous. I'm proud I held out. My boundary worked. I left around midday, perplexed.

I'm calming down and deciding how to spend my day or so of leave left. At home, at the farm, being a mum, unrushed, considering my absolute limits ahead. Regroup, despite the guarantee that my phone will ring soon with the next draining staff need. My personal taser is reliable; my money's on yet another roster rearrange before the day's out.

Bring on the farm day ahead. The physical exertion that delivers momentary relief from the swinging fists of burnout, and the logical and visible progress are the closest I can get to a rewarding feeling right now. There's something cathartic about sweat, dirt and grass clippings before returning to civilisation.

To my disappointment, I have a few bars of service up there, but the mountain air dulls each taser hit. Without a doubt, this attempted micro-break is my way of proving to myself that staying in the role won't work. The burnout won't let up because there's minimal help to cover the overload. I'm also hopeless at easing off, let alone stopping. Reduced productivity disorientates me. Which way is up?

Regardless, I must shield myself whenever the impossible unloads onto my full desk. Remove some of the urgency. Don't give it life. Duck and dodge the dropping containers of consignment and stop delivering every time. It only invites more of the same.

I will make this work until I'm next annoyed and used up. Push forward and push back. If those around me respect fair limits, I can maintain this eternal plank hold for a while longer. To all appearances, I have it together, but I don't. Sideline the desperate thinking, refresh and return clear-headed. Fix some controls in place. Proceed at a pace conducive to a human being, restrict interruptions and abandon perfectionism. People-pleasing is futile when the burdens are inexhaustible. Even charities have budgets. Care, cut off, care again, cut off again. Work in progress.

21 May 2024

Broken but pushing

My first full weekday off. No meetings today—productive, grounding. A refreshing gift to be home with those I love. My outlook improves when my brain breathes a little.

When I return tomorrow, I will focus on one item at a time. Embrace this challenge despite competing priorities, requests for my help and people at me all day. I'm nervous about the magnitude combined with the ever-present distractions and temptations to please.

Despite the ongoing demands, find a confident no, plaster my *Please do not disturb* sign to my door more often, and trust that

I will get everything done. False self-assurance persists, a hollow echo in the face of genuine vulnerability.

While I strategise a way to achieve the unachievable, questions flick me in the arm. Am I tired or pushed too far, or am I angry about the reliance on me? Both a privilege and a trap. I worked to be here, to reach this high-perched nest. Others trust my ability, but expertise and knowledge are also my curse. There's no protection from the elements, and this lead post I strived to obtain leaves me more vulnerable with each gust. I give my all to outcomes and others. Is this healthy, or enhancing the suffering? I must be doing it wrong. How do I decrease the calls for my input so I can get to my work? What else can I remove?

On the topic of elimination, what if I got sick? I have no backup. What if this burnout thing takes me out? My discussions and prompts about succession and support meet with positive agreement, but also unsuitable nothings, or a *resource* that generates more work. Job sharing, outsourcing, dividing aspects of my role. Agreement follows, but plans—and not for lack of trying—fall short, or through. No one's fault; it's just the way it is.

The changing of minds is like a new and erratic flight path I'm struggling to track. One day I'm told we are flying to Hawaii, so I prepare the team for that, but we jet back to base to pick up the directions to Sweden without stopping to refuel. The unproductive zigzags keep me running to collect my baggage and bypass security to find my next seat. Strapped in for take-off must mean we will see this trip out, make it all the way in a single direction. Nope, instead we divert to yet another airport to top off this week's mystery flight.

As I locate the team members left behind because either they couldn't keep up or listened to the wrong jumbled, overlapping final-gate call, I redo the trip again, in reverse and land back in Australia, wishing I had amnesia so I could skip having to rationalise what just happened. This style of working, day in and day out, deserves its own time zone, a place where the constant jet lag and bone-deep exhaustion are advertised as highlights of the repetitive round trip.

Gripes aside, pay attention to what needs nurturing. Invest in my health, my family. Life needn't mirror everything everyone else wants. At least not every time. Boundaries, although shakier than my trembling hands, must hold and expand because they are how I miss the next flight.

27 May 2024

Grateful and deluded

Gratitude gifts perspective and sustains glimmers of hope. If I blink rapidly, I see them—those elusive but bright flickers of faith.

Thankful for healthy kids, moments with family in nature at the farm, and all that's carrying me. The enveloping warmth of the fire each night too—thanks, babe.

Accompanying my gratitude is a high-strung tension that circles a bold red ring around my reality. What will hit me next? For a methodical planner, repeated exposure to operating on the fly turns my glimmer blinks into an involuntary eye twitch. There's no limit, nothing too absurd to add on top of everything else. I'm not my moderator, yet I'm responsible for so much. I must taper any immediate reactions to the flow of requests as I languish in my office when dark falls, struggling to catch up after another day that scurried away. Nights are my window. However, the end of the standard day is when the team passes by for one last trivial interruption. Well intentioned and friendly, but rarely helpful. They go home and I stay back, again. My colleagues impart the best advice yet. "Don't stay too late. You work too hard." To be fair, they are not privy to the entourage I just farewelled because this conga line moves through in department groups.

As the well-meaning line leaves my office, I worry about what's coming next. I have the schedule covered and execute with precision, a preparedness honed over years. But it's the surprise of the frivolous, regular and illogical pop-up tasks that shelve the important work and put me on a tangent to oblivion. The repeated full refund on any progress made is as fun as Christmas shopping from scratch in late December. Anyway, I do as I'm asked, understanding that disruption comes with transition. We are all trying. *The frustrating encounters will pass*. Make this my sleep whisper for a few nights. We'll get there.

Remember: boundaries and single-tasking. Too many first concerns not of my making mean I achieve less. Focus in order not to fail (hmm, do I need to fail?). Whatever, I'm focusing on positivity as the burden doubles down. Repeat that mantra to myself and don't forget to smile! I have much to action if I'm going to take my life back. It will be a great week. I *will*… leave in time to make it home before the boys are asleep; ensure the unimportant doesn't consume the days; delegate and direct drama away from my seat; resist the lure of perfection; tolerate less across the board; protect my wellbeing while I deliver; and partake only where necessary, because exuding a helpful and obliging attitude leads to more work. Self-preservation comes first.

And to round out my pep-talk—advocate for yourself. Hold back tears of desperation (crying on the way home counts); don't feed the brute of overwhelm. *The frustrating encounters will pass*, or I'll find the nerve to leave.

Part Two

Change

30 May 2024

I'm doing it

Today marks the first step towards the rest of my life. Today I chose life.

With relief, I reinstated my resignation and confirmed my need to leave. I'm doing it! Change is the only path forward, regardless of the decade and a half I invested here.

"So proud of you," my family repeat, revealing that they share my relief. I need only survive the next month and a bit. There's an end in sight. Keep charting towards that lighthouse.

My new superiors understood my decision (thank you!), and I wish them every success. They are contributors, but not the cause of my stress. They're just the next people in line needing me to deliver and showing appreciation each time I do. That's the job. The new approach to business feels enthusiastic and well intentioned, yet anxiety-inducing. Not wrong, but the wrong environment for me. The request to stay means a lot, but I must select differently. I used the word *no*! This is me letting people down. Day one.

With this comes many thoughts. So many thoughts about past actions and future choices…

What will I say to my team? As the leader who will soon leave them, this sits heavy, but I'll figure it out over the coming weeks, like everything else.

In the same way giving got me everywhere I thought I aspired to be, was it also the final straw? What cemented my suspicions that things were not alright, before and beyond the initial mention of burnout? A single event or burnout by a thousand paper cuts? Was it the insomnia, the depletion, the weekends in my office or spending Easter labouring alone because the sale deadline was approaching?

For sure, toiling for months to preserve vital initiatives through the changeover, followed by conflicting directives to move in opposite directions long-term, contributed too. No part of it aligns or sits well. Removing myself is the nobler move.

On further reflection, maybe the decider played out earlier in March during that glaring moral dilemma six weeks before settlement when Jackson relied on oxygen and endured a five-night hospital stay, courtesy of *Mycoplasma pneumoniae*.

Yep, that week from hell confirmed there was no backup, horrible circumstances or not. My job or my family—what comes first? Closing my eyes in the emergency department chair ahead of our 1 a.m. transfer to the paediatric ward, panic flooded me. Tomorrow would be like every other day. Frantic, striving to meet multiple targets as I balanced on my tightrope—and that was before adding the hospital stay. Working to target while being the unintentional bullseye for overload summarised March 2024's example of self-neglect.

So stupid—after night one on the hospital couch, I swapped places with Steven and headed to work. My heart cracked. This pain lingers. I failed as a mother that day, the morning I disregarded my maternal pull to be with my sick child. Incorrect, unnatural and wrong. I couldn't be there the whole time, despite longing to be. *Couldn't* has no place in my future.

"Take a couple of days, whatever you need," said past directors, more than once. In vain, I engineered later starts so I could be at the hospital as much as possible, but I had no cover. I should have sought help earlier. They would've obliged had I spoken up about my expanding workload and distress. But I hadn't, and I didn't. I told myself I was okay and accepted my responsibility. My broken record of excuses for my busy job played on.

Deluded and with eyeballs hanging out of my head, I worked like an idiot to meet the many deadlines on that hospital side-sleeper bed. From 4 a.m. I tapped away at the laptop keys ahead of tag-teaming with Steven. My fond memories of smiley Mr. Leo savouring the rotation of doting grandparents at his beck and call and his swift hands swiping the hospital jelly improved everything. At least Leo was living his best life.

Difficult or otherwise, I recall only parts of those days, but the shame remains. Jackson noticed me racing in and out between his crying and pleading with the nurse to remove the oxygen from his inflamed nose. An oxygen infusion and saline drip would've been beneficial for me too. If anything, to mandate me to his bedside.

I'm so sorry, Jackson, my brave boy. Despite maintaining a constant presence between us, I could've done better.

From today onward, I promise I will. With guilt at the rudder, my compass was busted, malfunctioning, and I was unable to distinguish the forest for the trees. I know that now. I also knew it then. That's what hurts the most—the deep undercurrents of regret that punish as they drag a person out to sea. Fortunately, the island where self-forgiveness and renewal await, like juicy coconuts hanging from the palms, isn't far off. I'm breast-stroking with the changing tide that leads to that shore. It's also home to that lighthouse.

There's hope already, and beyond my sad reality is an out-of-focus glimpse of my once marvellous life. I must hug change and hold on tight to the unfamiliar uncertainty ahead. A different ocean swim.

I'm unsure what's next but I trust it will be kinder than this. What do I want in the future? A situation where my career is not the entirety of life. Take comfort: freedom and release are coming. Embrace this meaningful shift in the right direction. Plan something fun with the family for soon after I finish. Mark this beginning and don't look back. An island getaway might be nice!

1 June 2024

Taking life back

By the creek in the forest, I am almost out of the woods. The birds, the rich scent of the damp cool earth, add to the green and calm. Trickling water over river rocks consoles; alone equals peace. Home is my favourite place.

Enjoy our secret garden. Don't think about the next role. It will come as I mend all that's frayed. First rebuild, work through, become whole again. Navigating this next period is all I have to do. My farm gloves and machete could be helpful to forge an obvious track, beyond the thick and thorny undergrowth and restricting branches to the inviting path, my yellow brick road. I'm not sure how I got here, confined in my lonely panic room. Did I create the angst within, or am I waking up to the nonsense I shouldered for so long? Difficult to call, and it doesn't matter. In this desperate and damaged place, not grabbing change now would be a mistake, a suffocation of what spirit remains.

My position, it's complex and taxing, with volumes of moving parts. No matter how organised I am or how long I grind, work pins me to the wall. Every email and knock at my door reveals the latest issue or changing industry-wide scheme requiring my waning attention, demanding I stop, drop, run and roll to someone's non-urgent aid.

Everything takes a piece of me. I can't move fast enough through the crowd of needy bodies to fill my cup. *In need* takes on a destructive nature, similar to a gift gone wrong. I hurry, but I'm heavy and sore, trudging on in my responsibility-loaded boots.

In other words, my soul hurts. However, it's easing because I have a plan, an exit and an end to my approaching emotional flatline. As I regain consciousness, my many tiny life errors offer understanding.

At last, my long-acting, people-pleasing anaesthetic is wearing off, and I'm no longer oblivious to the complicit removal of boundaries. As I wake from the period of my life that extracted my gauge for conventional limits, brightness shines from above. Flashbacks of where I went wrong, the ordeal where I traded freedom for money, where getting the job done left me paralysed down one side, are clear. My paralysis around family, health and happiness is consequential yet temporary. My prognosis is good, and change is my chance at a promising outcome.

For now, my prediction is that my power-walking pace around the surgery would qualify for an Olympic heat. I tested my speed and impact ratio a couple of months back. Moving at my standard efficient pace towards the front of house, I was suddenly knocked to the ground. My teammate, who had been coming around the corner, shared my shock at our blind-spot collision.

As I hit the floor that afternoon, I broke the water cooler and my false sense of security on my descent. We'd finished for the day, so no patient witnessed the manager injure herself at the doctor's surgery! I sat motionless on the soggy floor, holding back full-blown tears. Far past done, with hours of work ahead before I could glide home in my usual haze, I located my legs, pride and the spirit to stand, clean up and assure everyone that I was fine. I had to be fine. "What did you guys need my help with again?" I asked. I hobbled back to my room, where I had a brief chance to unleash the water behind my eyes in private before the next task.

Lots of my days play out this way, metaphorically speaking. The sad common denominator is, I get back up. But I don't want to spend my one life racing around busy corners. No one would give their entire self unless it made them wealthy or if the business were their own. I'm operating in a way that dilutes my effectiveness and welfare. I no longer accept the burden and no longer want to feel owned. Transfer my skills while embracing freedom and choice, despite the many questions I have left to ponder by the water cooler.

Question: Who am I? Do I even have dreams? Answer: Piece myself together, one broken fragment at a time. Bones heal with rest and protection, so I will too.

Question: How do I let go? How can I adapt my drive for constant productivity? What will restore my humanity? Answer: Control over my time and input, rest and a chance to focus on an intellectual project. Interests unrelated to work are great. Find some.

Of all the queries I am yet to solve, I'm bolting down a firm choice—to leave this life behind. Proud! I achieved the desired results and earned a reputation of quality, now I choose to move on. Any further energy spent worrying is a waste of air and minutes. Be careful not to land here again. That's valuable lesson number one of this experience. Time will help if I allow it, if I release and shed concerns about leaving my solid yet concluding past behind. That's learning number two. Profound. Take life back into my hands.

2 June 2024

Preparing for release

S taring up at the ceiling mid-examination during my skin check today, the same question pops up: *Am I the only one who thought my situation passed as normal?*

"How's everything going?" asks my doctor while checking for any worrying moles or spots.

How to answer this without breaking down? Say it like it is: resignation, struggling, burnout, figuring out my emotions. He'd see this every day. Say something, share your news. This pause is worse. The words tumble out, and surprisingly, confirmatory acceptance arrives fast. "It sounds like you're doing the right thing," he says. "And how are you emotionally?"

"I'm alright." Semi-honest is my best bet to avoid tears and not take up too much of his day. My white-lie response fools no one, and the bags under my eyes give away more than my unconvincing words, but it doesn't matter.

"I can arrange some sessions with someone for you if you need." His caring smile, free from pressure, reassures me that I can reach out. However, the only therapy I crave is time alone. If I could sleep long enough to dream, I'd see myself embarking on a boring version of Cheryl Strayed's solo therapy walk from *Wild*, minus the camping bit. My take would involve trekking the winding tracks of the secluded state forest behind our house by day and returning each afternoon to be the best mum in the world.

I'll miss the work I do, but the difficulty getting to it causes the stress—perfectionism too. The scale of the handover may scare suitable replacements away. Regardless, I push on with full effort to the end.

It's no surprise that transferring my know-how of practice operations to a giant categorised spreadsheet is like penning a guidebook on how to make it to Mars while caring for a litter of puppies. Lucky I'm doing it in my spare time, on the weekends between football games and afternoons of scooter drop-ins at the skate park. There's nothing quite like sitting on a rug watching the boys ride while plotting a survival plan for the next man. The bull ant bite on my ankle reminds me that a lot still stings and welts. As usual, Jackson's sweaty cuddles at each water top-up make everything okay. "Hey, Mum." Loving arm around my shoulder, water gulp. "Bye, Mum." More reminders of why I'm doing this.

I'm a smidge shy of certain no one will read my spreadsheet masterpiece, but that's not my problem. There's much to include, do, detail and explain while in continuous motion. Out of sympathy for the ambitious worker who will fill my spot, I offered support for soon after I fly away. Burnout doesn't excuse me from doing right, or from everything else I have to pull off in the weeks ahead.

Disclosing my overdue surrender to change to my doctor and friends is beneficial. Clarity will return with time. They make it sound simple and reassuring; the context and comfort sit well. Facing burnout—as in, doing something about it—is my attempt at braving my fear of judgement, failure and healthy detachment from my all-consuming professional life. Change requires replacing the weight in my pack. Needless weight out, rescue equipment in. This is me owning my downward spiral, no longer opting to exacerbate my pain. Instead, I'll choose differently and scatter some seeds of hope on my journey back to wellness. Of course, my loose plan includes more than throwing around handfuls of sunflower kernels. I hope they'll sprout, but I've experienced enough to know that hope alone produces meek results. My said plan involves taking a month or two, or more, off, courtesy of my stash of accrued leave I failed to use because everyone needed me. Afterwards, I'll embark on a leisurely and intentional search for what fits. Attach no conditions to having a break. Make it a season of rest, a true holiday.

In the months ahead, I'll fill the days with all that's gentle and positive. I'll savour being alone and bid farewell to the harrowing worry that tenants my mind. Goodbye. Once stress packs up and moves abroad, I'll have opportunities to explore alternatives, to determine what I want, to do whatever I please.

A break is coming. I will be fine. I'm open to possibilities and confident I'll achieve and earn while living well. If my wellbeing improves, that's enough. The rest will find me as I release and soar.

6 June 2024

When personal shutdown feels like madness, but it's not

The changing instructions are so confusing, I can't keep up. Functioning is difficult, unfamiliar territory. Is it burnout or my situation that's the problem at this point? My other recurring question—am I being punked? Is this even happening? There's no order to how I have to operate. Surreal. Thoughts of banging my head on my desk instead of cradling it in my hands in disbelief resonate as reasonable. If I could knock myself unconscious without leaving a mark or hide behind my office door to avoid the next head that pops in, I would.

More new tasks roll through, threatening my progress as I complete as much as possible in the time remaining. Per my usual commitment-to-the-cause approach, I'm getting through a lot, but shutdown is close. Who will attend to the volume once I'm gone? I care so much. More than I should.

Then there's my recurring thoughts of failure surrounding my choice to walk away, despite the certainty that failing myself any longer would be the ultimate fault. An Oscar nomination for most convincing performance of outward composure in an emotional nightmare is likely if I perform on. I was unaware a person could fade to an array of lacklustre shades of beige (not the stylish capsule wardrobe kind). This dull colour palette of exhaustion is not my best look. Good thing I'm tapping out prior to awards season.

The questions from my team about why I'm leaving are difficult to face as well. I repeat honest responses without saying it all. Too many opinions and too much information won't help me or them. My universe is already spinning, processing this new stage of strange. I want to stop feeling. But because that's not an option, I'm embracing the relief that meets me as each day completes. The finish date on my calendar inches closer. I persevere, tangled in the sticky webs that overthinking constructs. Disappointed that I gave up; I'm not the kind of person who gives up. It's a bizarre sensation, relinquishing something other than myself for once.

As my confidence declines, a battered impostor takes up residence in my skin. My pre-burnout capabilities are now reflections of my best, threads of a past existence. Feeling this low warrants my decision. The void in my veins shakes me with concern. I held firm in this agonising pattern for ages. Why? It is possible the impostor is my intuition, guiding me away, holding me up as it enquires. Not sure.

Change feels off at first until it makes sense and redirects life to a nicer place. Hopefully, that's what's unfolding. I made it here, through each extra surge of effort, beyond each challenge. Conquer this state of limbo with equal perseverance. Let the rest take care of itself. If anything, the hourly confirmations telling me to sprint rather than melt away are helpful. Continuous confirmatory gems verify it's my time to move on. Wrap it up and reject professional servitude for good.

Progress looks like declining the position another company offered today. These declines will remain my default response to everything except water, food and love from the boys—to clear the way and the webs, because the only position I'm up to is regaining some colour.

15 June 2024

Certainty matters and uncertainty incites fear

I'm certain yet uncertain of so much, but that's how this chapter of my story must read. Nothing will change otherwise.

Uncertainty's an unnerving playlist featuring strange compilations of fear and curiosity. However, despite my preference for neat reassurances, uncertainty and variety also give back.

I'm certain change is the only viable option, that things can improve. Prioritise health and family and be available for the boys. Burnout is dangerous: I'm certain of that too. An addiction to work is still an addiction. Limiting damage and protecting my peace is on me, another sure thing, as is knowing that walking away will revive my life.

I stand a chance if I deal with burnout the way I face other challenges. The odds swing my way. Historically, I've shown up and achieved more than I imagined, despite circumstances. Full effort with attention to detail coupled with a preparedness slick enough to organise a presidential campaign could serve here too.

I treat others as I would like to be treated. Turn that around, treat myself as I treat others, and this chapter has the potential to become a melody, where tribulation modulates into healing. Combine a relaxation soundtrack with a bit of pace and the storytelling of a country music song for a more moving sound. Draw from all I already am, all I possess, and use it to heal my life. My skills are ready and versatile, so use them to do right by myself rather than a job. Turn those skills inwards. That's the brief.

Create my own certainties within each doubt, reviewing the strong precedents as I go. Release worry, perfection, opinions and apologies and just be. Give weight to what nourishes and restores. I'll have time for that soon. Use uncertainty as motivation to construct an ideal life, the future I want—a certain reality where I'm home in time each night to share a meal. Burnout and uncertainty are my fears, but also my big chance.

25 June 2024

Frustrations and finish lines

This head cold is on the improve. I'm holding on, aware I can't rest yet. The end of my self-imposed toxic existence is materialising, taking shape with each shallow breath. The finish line is within reach. Don't lose sight.

Today, like every day, I will do what I can, accepting the impossibility of getting it all done. The pile and scope are enough to stampede a team of experienced staff, confirmed on repeat, not only by me. Masking the listlessness accompanying my exhaustion is unbearable; the punishing crescendoing sensitivity and frustration is too. I scream inside, and the volume's loud, my muscles tense, but no one hears my pleas—they're internal. My accommodating smile is the mirage I'm maintaining to uphold the illusion of coping, but it's shaky.

Despite the noise, thoughts of guaranteed better days ahead are all I have left to sustain the pace I must maintain. Not much further to go; this is the home straight, the brutal last leg. Finish on my feet.

Unfortunately, the communication coming my way would muddle anyone, I'm sure. Either that or I no longer understand business, English or both. It could be me, or part of the depletion. The lead position is difficult with decreasing control as my departure inches closer, but we are all doing our best, task by task. Handing over all I nurtured and contributed to hurts more than I imagined. I want out, but releasing everything I worked for is a loss, something precious slipping through my hands.

All I can do is keep moving through. I'll soon be past this red-flag situation. There will be more outside days, sunlight, and simplicity will mend my past mistakes. Give my all and then be free. These thoughts of freedom and a chance to rediscover my strengths and abilities provide much-needed direction. I'll not feel broken for long. Lost for a little while, yes, but I'll heal as light and life filter in. Everything signals it will be a different path, strengthened by the building anticipation as I close out each task. There's more for me than a perpetual state of burnout. This can't be it. I won't regret reclaiming my time and recovering from what my life has become.

I will soon step forward for me, free of a weight that I have little control over, no matter how diligently I work. Energy's low. No more slaving without pause and on repeat. Much of it I enjoyed. Hopefully, that doesn't make me the textbook definition of a lost soul, or naïve. I used myself, condoning and asking for it all. This fall and finish are on me. What comes next is too.

5 July 2024

Walking away to walk forward

Recent days have been a blur of work, goodbyes, handovers, late nights and appreciation from colleagues. I can't recall it in enough detail to make sense on the page. Not now, anyway. A lot of good happened, head-spinning stuff too, but it holds less relevance today because I'm done!

Today, I walked away. I completed my gruelling race. There's no sadness, only relief. I am numb.

So proud that I worked at full capacity, in every capacity, to the end. I stayed true to the determined but depleted athlete within. The odd but smooth last stretch made it easy to close the practice door behind me one last time tonight. I received a medal of complete confirmation that I'm doing the right thing—my greatest award yet.

On arrival home, my three smiling and cheering boys greeted me in the entryway as I staggered from the car with all my loot. Holding a congratulations sign, they welcomed me with enthusiastic applause. They clapped me in, the emotion I brushed aside all day saved for this moment. Hugs, tears, complete release. Squeezing their excited faces and sharing the joy is my celebration. I am here. Their elation humbled me as much as it welcomed me back into the fold.

Surrounded by love, I walked through the door and collapsed with a smile.

Part Three

Healing and the In-Between

9 July 2024

Beginnings

To my delight, on the other side of change is uneventful joy. Day four of my new situation is freedom—beginning. These first few days floating around home are a release.

Each morning, I'm bouncing out of bed to reread my hand-drawn congratulations card the boys held as a sign on my arrival home last week. It encapsulates my freedom and reads like a certificate of achievement, marking a turning point towards peace. Smiley faces saying *wow, good job*, shooting stars, bright pink hearts, mini thumbs-up drawings and an array of colour fill the page.

Congrats!

Fifteen-year accomplishment (underlined and spelled as a c o m p l e s h m e n t).

Congratulations for completing fifteen whole years of work. We know it was tough!

Congrats, we are all happy for you, that you can get some free time to yourself.

We all love you!!!!!!!!!!!!!!!!!!!!

Signed (they wrote the word signed and drew a purple arrow pointing to their names) *Jackson, Leo, Dad, Chase and Rusty pups.*

I plan to hang it on the wall soon to commemorate how right this new life is. Meanwhile, it commands the front spot in the middle of the dining table and in my heart, beside the arrangements of flowers and other symbols of thanks.

This is all normal enough, right? Who cares! Whatever's happening here is healthy. Plus, the house smells like a flower market. I keep stopping to touch the silky petals of support as I move between the rooms, feeling the positivity and openness for what's ahead between my fingers.

Already, my achievements in freedom include fun with my boys, some sleep and a full embrace of personal space. Simple comforts play out as extravagant indulgences multiple times per day. Who do I thank? In the last couple of days alone, there are anecdotes aplenty, endless giving joys, but I'll get them down a bit later. In this moment, I'm hugging my little house as I do the boys. At last, I get to be here, at ease. Nobody needs me every five seconds. This liberating game changer delivers beyond the release of all other restraints. This is how I will heal.

The opposite of anxiety is the awe that hope is introducing to the mix. These early inklings of recovery mimic the flood of endorphins after an intense run. I didn't imagine this. It's real and mine. Why did I permit distress as the default? I'm unsure how I ignored the burning inside for so long. What for? Varying perspectives come to mind, but I'm not ready to explore them all yet. It's too soon to give air or attention to the remnants of past stress or to feeling lost here and there. Besides, for now, I'm relishing my congrats card and a little free time.

11 July 2024

Evolve or repeat

This choice, this in-between, is what every part of me reaches for. I'm different, lighter. Anxiety fades with each sunrise as the breakfast platter of subtle resolutions presents itself. I have a say over my existence. The air's pure here; it affirms life. I was correct. All in, embracing this leap is the best way. My self-preservation experiment is a cold plunge for the psyche, an arctic shock back to life. Healing is happening. That's what's in the air. There's mending going on inside. My body's relaxing, my shoulders releasing below my ears for the first time since age twenty-five, the tightness and tension easing.

The minor pleasures are the best part. Freedom is having time, welcoming stillness and appreciating my cosy home.

And productivity without racing tastes like some exotic elixir that cultivates calm. Action's important, but it's action alongside renewal as I find my bearings in this grassy meadow. No part of me questions whether I did the right thing. I'm home, and my new rose-coloured glasses are the real deal.

In this season, I can be all the kids need. No one else holds control. Present, right here, taking my chance to experience this new frequency free from the ache that gripped my chest. To clarify, I can breathe and see.

It's all clear. I endured and sustained the crippling intensity without question. Year in, year out, I accepted it, calling it progression. I correlated overwork with success. It worked for me, each time I progressed to the next gigantic task with achievement in my wake. However, one-dimensional achievement falls short of genuine victory, more so when it demolishes your spirit, home and health. This should have been obvious.

The growing strength in each moment and tranquillity in every interaction validate the goodness. Lean into relaxed progress. That's it. Let the relief amplify as it mends and never again give yourself away.

12 July 2024

Happy Friday, for real this time

This is a good place. Here, in our backyard fernery, perched on the fallen mossy log by the creek. The sun's filtering between the trees, warming my face as it peeks through. It's all shades of light down here in the grove. The song of the whipbirds and the pups exploring creates a background hum. Noise unlike before. A Friday afternoon of a different kind.

My exhausting late-night finishes are over. Instead, strolls along the creek bed are part of this new tempo I'm crafting. At least for a little while. Butterflies are everywhere every day, a beauty I've not witnessed until now. This afternoon's friendly monarchs come so close, as if they want to land on my nose as I internalise nature's gifts by the creek. In the forest and at the athletics carnival this morning, I'm bottling my gratitude as freely as it flows.

"Mumma, you're here!" Jackson beamed as I found him in the colourful crowd. With my newfound present-mum pride, I was there and available for fun.

Locating Leo was easy thanks to his golden locks curling out from under his hat. Too cool to come to me, he flashed his all-teeth grin and sent a wave in my direction while taking his place at the starting line with his friends. *Hey Mum, watch me*—I'm sure that's what he mouthed. I'll take it.

I'll take all of this, being a mum without having to arrange time or seek permission to choose my kids. For once, I didn't miss the carnival and I let no one down. I had no time limit, nothing else going on, and no phone dominating my life. Today I'm their mum, not a distraction in sight. My agenda is them, and they notice.

I endured for so long that I forgot what it's like to design how my days play out. What a waste. There's an upside to unused leave and years of investment property hustles—the financial means to allow an extended break. More gratitude, to even have this available.

In time, the right opportunity will find me. It already has. Burnout's shown up as a difficult and unlikely ally in forcing my necessary exit, one I may not have made alone. On this side of change, burnout's part of my remedy, offering feedback that solves.

Fresh frame of reference aside, slowing down is odd. Unreal, almost. Sometimes I reflect to make sense of what happened. My sleepless months and the vertigo associated with figuring it out explain a lot. So too my strained positivity and the kidding-myself mindset I personified to sugarcoat my demise. Either way, it's sad to comprehend my desperation a few weeks back. It's okay, though.

More overdue happiness returns on this first free Friday afternoon amongst the ferns. Life's good; everything signals so. I'm brave as I start to live again.

15 July 2024

Reversing the damage burnout and I inflicted involves unpicking tapestries of behaviour, a delicate job for the creator of the cloth, the seamstress who interlaced the threads. Only I can pretty this picture.

Lying here tucked up in bed, those dizzying, weaved experiences are hazy, but my intuition's not. Neither is the recent and regular presence of rainbows. Between the rainbows and butterflies, are they transpiring to create a new piece of art? This theory at least provides an excuse to postpone the untangling for now.

Three rainbows coloured my path in the two days after finishing up at work. A double rainbow even, in my face as I walked with Mum and the boys through the sun shower to meet Dad at the half marathon finish line that weekend. What's on the other side? In a way, this suspended reality's a prelude to the entrance to sustained peace and joy. Head there!

Today, I asked for verification beyond my knowing that all is as it should be. Life's too good to be true. I'm experiencing an openness to both spirituality and uncertainty about the future, but no fear (yet). To stay on theme, I chose a rainbow as ongoing proof that this will work out. So silly, looking for messages in rainbows, but another part of me suspects that out-of-the-ordinary things appearing on repeat means something. Believe in something over nothing.

Within hours, mention of rainbows are all over my phone. Random but auspicious, so I'll keep my eyes open. I'm going to be fine—better than fine. I'm listening and want to be receptive to more. This is me welcoming the many questions and lessons. Please come in. I'm doing my best to spot the subtle guidance, the little nudges and reassurances. Many thus far, such as *the Universe*, it reaches beyond a job and stress, and a *nervous system* is more nuanced than being nervous or embodying a system that's flawed. I'm regrouping with rest as I tiptoe forward with joy as the goal. I forgot how comforting elation is. The days are different, each a deluxe personal interlude I get to explore.

My most recent and satisfying milestone adding to my glow? I now sleep, no longer afraid to climb into bed. Slumber's serene wonderland is worth noting. Sleep and privacy are magnifying the array of uplifting things at my disposal, details I missed. I'm not alone anymore, but I'm blissfully alone, another beautiful paradox of recovery. Still a tad restless about the changes, but free. It's a rapid turnaround. My complete surrender to and trust in change has a lot to do with it. Or, it could be the release from overwork, a reality I assembled, normalised and decorated with excuses. I forgot I had wings, or a choice.

Burnout was that deafening plea for change. My body yelled as I pushed the symptoms aside until they grew obvious and loud. A message. Apparently, my body's memos can also be pleasant and confirmatory when everything is as it should be, when I listen.

I have goals, but I'm unsure. My current definition of success is a Monday afternoon at home while the kids play, smelling the smoke wafting from neighbourhood chimneys as the sun fades and the aroma of banana muffins baking in the oven. Yes, I'm on holidays and this can't last, but these small moments, my weekday afternoons, are special. The days are mine.

Success is freedom of choice. It exists in the silence and solitude of achievement without constant interruption, and experiences with my family—they're the gold. Add to that weekends spent in the garden, and the means to pillar a modest life removed from frantic pace and frantic thought. What feels correct will guide my next decisions. A smaller part-time role is in my future, so I can direct energy towards the boys, the farm and writing long-term. No pressure. When I'm ready, I'll see where this idea leads, likely to a spectacular other side. This side of broken is where my history and imperfections reorientate to form outcomes more valuable than any straight-line repair. Writing is part of the healing; it is the healing. If this is my way forward, it will present in full colour, like the rainbows.

26 July 2024

Content

A pleasant life—this is it.

An afternoon in the garden following a morning pottering around home—that's all it takes. Mundane yet so satisfying. Can healing be this straightforward? Amid the towering green trees, book in hand, I marvel at the breeze rustling the leaves. High above, the branches sway like contemporary dancers across a stage of clouds. The rising smoke and crackles from the backyard fire pit add to the show. Content is an understatement.

This reality is real, and it's mine. I keep saying it because I can't believe it. I'm filled with enthusiasm for my future and this moment. Presence is a gift. It's comfort in each moment, enhanced by engagement and a dash of awe, sprinkled with delicate edible petals for effect. Overall, the possibilities following breakdown captivate and intrigue. Along my way, I'm unearthing the unexpected privileges and enlightenments that can bud and bloom from pain, like fossicking and finding diamonds and gemstones as I go. They must come with change. I purchased my freedom. At last, I chose myself. Keep stepping in this direction.

For starters, my renewed liberties granted me a five-day girls' trip to Bali for my friend Eva's fortieth. What a novelty to venture beyond my office and the car, to be available. Not the traditional *Eat, Pray, Love* odyssey, although I got them all in. Eat, yes; love, yes, because I have the greatest friends; and I guess I prayed when that savvy cyber terrorist hacked my account within hours of arrival. That eight-thousand-dollar welcome scam wasn't a joke.

In a way, my lingering exhaustion prevented me from worrying about it to my usual degree, or much at all. New for me. After my prayers/profanities, calls to the bank and a few drinks, Bali gave back. Even the terrifying ferry ride through rough, angry black waters to that overrated Indonesian island for a day of snorkelling didn't dampen things. I'll own being the tourist who took out the prize for the most *oh shits* on the perilous boat ride back to safety and hackers. I'm alive, my money's back in my account, and I loved my stay. The significance: I had time to go, I felt free (and a little scared), and I retrieved a semi-laid-back side of myself I forgot existed.

Although it's temporary, I'm adamant the itinerary for the rest of my life will be close to this enchanting period of pause and tour of emotional discovery. No more boat trips, though. I will choose sagaciously ahead. Comprehending that living involves more than work is valuable beyond measure. I'm repairing. Change is working out, and there's no need to worry anymore. Life has me. I survived burnout and that boat for a reason.

Holidays, exhaustion and self-discovery aside, the conflict is gone and my path ahead is up to me. I control my approach and how I tread, rather than reacting to the next chaotic initiative thrown my way. My dodgeball days are done. Challenges come, but they don't consume my thinking, and they never needed to. I have all kinds of capable up my sleeve.

I accept I don't have or need all the answers. The unknown now sparks a fondness. Who knew that I (a perfectionist) would feel unchained in my age of alluring uncertainty? The more days I spend in the garden at ease, the more I relax. This in-between requests only that I trust in the journey.

As I progress on, my universe is richer the more I remove. Belief and optimism exist again, and panic is gone. I'm free from obligation to anyone other than myself and those I love. This is success, the many lovely things in my life. I've made it.

Pen to paper

Back by the fire pit at sunset, the evening's cool but not cold—balanced. The mood of the night matches my feelings of lost but good—*good lost*.

Contemplation of then, now and what could be nudges open various doors. The incomplete rooms of emotion behind each frame the structure of the house. They contribute to the whole. The writing, reading and processing prompt questions and observations, enhancing the progress and quality of my internal home. It's meditative.

My lasting ambition spills onto the page most days. The rhythm in the writing is an outlet, a means of being conscious of the changes swirling within. Pen to paper offers direction—navigation to the inlet ahead of the safe harbour on the horizon. The outline of the safeguarded port appears as a place of ongoing refuge, with ample protection from the nonstop demands of open seas. A haven for healing and securing provisions.

In the same way, my journals settle nerves about the mysteries and uncharted passages ahead. They elicit admiration and approval of what I can choose to embrace next and how best to turn my wheel. The messy flow of words comes with ease. Spiral-bound notepads at the helm have extraordinary power and pull.

Before, I couldn't choose. Life kept increasing its incline, taking me to the edge of nowhere. I struggled to find sense in the hours that made up the days. Each became a haze of overlapping service to the unimportant. Not my voyage, so to speak.

This midlife wake-up call isn't a setback, instead it offers recognition that I used myself up for no benefit of my own. It was like walking a shorter plank every day. Sacrifice is no more my way of life. I'm fortunate to have this restorative active respite, the chance to withdraw and retreat to a place of shelter.

Writing makes healing tangible. There's an enriching and vital selfishness that surrounds personal preservation and improvement. It's that fundamental and humanistic self-regard, the one I released as the needs of others leapfrogged to the top of the pile. The writing puts me back up there, word by word. I'm sheepish about recording this next observation, especially in my journal: I long wrote for a professional case or cause and viewed journalling as meaningless, reserved for the self-involved. But hey, here I am, flourishing despite the irony.

I made a lot of mistakes. Engulfed in all that contributed to burnout—my workload, the perpetual demands that overtook wellbeing—I justified many wrongs in the pursuit of success. Confirmation of life equalled the repeated intrusions. Everyone needed me all the time to do all the things in quick succession and often all at once. Bending to fit, contorting to deliver, exceeding limits, I was the lunatic playing a continual lone game of Twister in a tornado in the middle of a freeway. With a smile and styled hair, of course.

I received five-star reviews for my ability to complete everything while bettering outcomes (for everyone else). To all accounts, I was winning, and the praise egged me on. But my stint starring as the resident glutton for punishment in the healthcare version of *Australian Survivor* now lives in the archives, shelved for good.

My new existence is more candid memoir than survival-themed directive, exploring updated iterations of what I classify as confirmation of a glorious life. It's softer, featuring high fives from the boys and safe versions of Twister, Snap and Memory, for a start.

Keep trusting this well lit yet ironic journalling path. Let the flat days be what they are. The lulls are novel, but necessary. They too contribute to the process of moving through. Inspiration and loving verifications visit in these pauses. I think of Gran often these days. I miss her. Strong and independent, she valued the basics, achieving much in her one hundred years. Her family, garden, books and pets were her affirmations, alongside introversion and rest. As an advocate for early nights, meals packed with homegrown veg and a glass or two of whatever warms you, Gran lived a wholesome life. I'm thankful for her solid example. Pleased, too, that I no longer operate as a robot with a pulse.

30 July 2024

Observing while restoring

Definition of *fortunate*: Opportunities to unwind, inhale and replenish after long holding my breath.

To do: keep breathing deep.

Observation: being a nobody is *the best*. I notice points in time now. This is new too. There's much to enjoy—the beginning of each day, quiet becoming the default, and the capacity to care for my family. Self-determination is an upgrade from "too busy to breathe". Time is also relative to the load.

I've come a long way, no longer speeding through tasks while adding more and standing on my head. Sometimes I glorify the highs of the productivity I'm accustomed to, but my list of accomplishments is enough for now. I'm not erasing them. Instead, there's solace in no longer forcing myself to perform in a residency show every day and night, whether unwell, overloaded or otherwise.

My latest frontier leaves me with more than mere scraps of myself. Life's value surpasses any pay cheque or conditions-attached accolade. Moderation in everything, except faith in love and belief that what's emerging may prove superior to any plan I could conjure. The racing anxiety and other dilemmas remain in my past. Distance helps.

With performance acrobatics and headstands removed, I get to evaluate how I feel. My mind's receptive, clear and vibrant again. Simplicity's working—"ungoverned and selective" reads my byline, and fulfilled is the mood.

The sunny side of change illuminates the weaknesses in my old patterns, exposing what didn't work. It opens my eyes, reducing the distortion and dangers I missed and ignored along my burnt-out and breathless way. Each day I'm stronger than the last as focus and respiration return to my refreshing little life. It's insignificant and low-key but adorned with inspiring charm and openness to the light that's touching everything. May this beaming warmth restore and assure as it transforms.

All of this also defines *fortunate*.

5 August 2024

Welcome, pink butterfly

Our Hamilton Island holiday is more than I expected. Likewise, peace presents itself as an impressive scene, one I didn't foresee, part of a dream.

I'm inhaling the cool, fresh gusts here on the protected, palm-lined beach. Few people, no lines, and the prime sun lounges unoccupied—oh, the advantages of low-season travel! After our morning of sailing, I'm returning to my lounge perched on a bed of crushed coral, perfect. Steven and the boys chart on, manoeuvring the beach club catamaran in the bay. They are all smiles, Steven steering and their hands skimming through the water while they mimic the moves and seriousness of the tanned pathfinders in *Moana*. I need a little more colour to coordinate with my fast-moving, bronzed family crew. I'm working on it. Between basking, reading and the catamaran entertainment, I'm good.

Fun—that's today. The breathtaking vistas of ocean, sky and nearby islands morph into each other, extending as far as I can see. Each afternoon, the tropical air invigorates us to play back-to-back rounds of sand-under-your-feet island ping-pong. Competitive table master Leo makes up the rules as we go.

For these reasons, I am free. The island getaway helps, but generally and genuinely, I'm free. On holiday with my boys and no laptop. My work is to rest, to let my hair soak up the salty breeze and to watch the Olympics in bed with the kids while someone else makes dinner. The women's skateboarding coverage is their latest obsession. "Mum, let's stay up late to see more," they ask. "We're going for the youngest skater for the gold. She's epic."

This dream state lifts me higher than the island climb Jackson and I conquered yesterday. Poor kid, it was a decent climb to the top of the world.

To add to it all, I dreamed of a pink butterfly. The ability to sleep and dream again is one of many desires coming true. My sunrise curiosity led me to investigate the meaning of the coloured butterfly that hovered as I slept. Smiling, I pressed my eyes closed when my search revealed the symbolism. Freedom, growth and transformation ride on the wings of the pink butterfly. Appropriate.

These shifts in mindset and awareness welcome only more good, a happiness that promotes greater happiness. Similar to the industrious cockatoos that run the island who dominate sunset drinks and nibbles on the balcony each afternoon, redefine playing for keeps and duplicate on demand.

Because of it all, my heart's full. I'm growing as I change and return to a beautiful baseline. I've already surpassed *fine*, and verification comes in therapeutic doses. My attention's back on too. This is the return of my body's vital signs. Every day there's something returned to remind me I'm featuring in the right story. My own.

6 August 2024

In our temporary island home sitting high over the reef, palms and sand, we enjoy respite from the sun. Our morning of play and lazing deserves an afternoon to match.

Today's status report from paradise declares that my pasty office white complexion is, like burnout, a thing of the past. One month since my life changed, and everything's transforming with the moving tide. My days and weeks again hold meaning. The leisure between what was and what might be next provides a valuable phase of rest and retreat. I can relish moments because I'm around for them. Truth in action: I'm on this holiday and not at work!

For the reasons above and more, I'm savouring the present as lovingly as possible, despite thinking about what could be next.

I could have used this endearing embrace earlier in the year. Earlier self-care would've helped. I'm making up for it.

Just like that, the past is back there, done. It had to happen like this. Value and difficulty, break and elevate, give and take. Some opposites belong and remain together. I see that now. Some days I awake stunned from it all, but mostly in awe that I slept. I've gone back in time, to former years where boundless sleep is a given. The before babies, toddlers and real responsibility type of rest. I write about it a lot because it's foundational, part of the turnaround in me, the basis for a breakthrough.

Similar to the end of insomnia, not performing to my limit day and night is a strange but welcome development. It's all I knew— there was no end to someone needing something. Month after month, I'm reflecting on the days I endured. Darting from task to interruption to call to email to meeting to problem to project and back again. Momentum, my motto, transitioning so fast, my erratic pulse jumping rope quicker than my legs. Persistent over-load distorted everything. Geez, at one point I even pictured a troll under my bed keeping me wired and awake. That wasn't long ago.

That being achievable, anything is possible. A basic premise, but it may hold the answers to lasting change. Envision working differently as I proceed on my way. A job that allows me to be a mum—does it exist? Likely yes, but I wedged myself so far under paperwork and people that I didn't consider it. I would never have entertained a step down, but post-burnout me thinks otherwise. Embody change—that's the entire purpose of this stage, isn't it? If anything, it settles the fears I have about returning to work. Hmm, this less-money-for-more-freedom concept won't go away, a trade I must explore, despite the time I put in to become someone impressive. Less is different, but it honours my promise to foster an enhanced capacity for life.

To my type-A personality's amazement, existing in the short-term and flowing with the breeze is a treat. My plans had to be fluid and my outlook temporary to outlast burnout. I have questions about the future, but the short-term enhances the possibilities to heal. This is my leeway to explore and to take care, to entertain prospects that were not on my organised agenda before. Relief that I'm unwilling to throw myself straight back into the vortex of a senior role. Voluntary imprisonment no longer makes sense. Nothing's a mistake, except questioning whether it was alright to choose my needs.

It's a progression, one where gratitude builds and forward is my focus. I'm at a different stage of burnout—fragile, but hopeful and so satisfied. Either way, I'm bettering my situation as I reverse the impact. From desperate to here, sharing ice cream, island buggy rides and chilled beach mornings with the kids. I'm progressing through and appreciating the strengths that helped me stay standing. I rallied at my lowest, my most important push yet.

11 August 2024

Good doesn't need to be hard

Sunday afternoons are now free from nervous anticipation and intrusive annoyances. My time belongs to me, ease increases, clarity too. I can think again. The fog's disappearing. This is my chance to marvel at the valley instead of navigating the ranges with an entourage in tow. The shadows cast by the peaks set the mood—aspirational.

Past ideals of who I have to be fade, loosen, relax. I'm exploring options that could maintain the giving life alternations that burnout compelled me to adopt on the fly. It's acceptable to point time and self towards things I like. Not everything needs to be a hike uphill to be worthwhile. Our days regenerating the farm without pressure reveal that worthy effort needn't be a battle.

I hauled my fair share up gnarly inclines and received recognition for it, which I relied on as confirmation, my next marker on the track, my cue to go harder. I lived for the summits. They were as frequent as they were rewarding. Victory feels good, despite the toll. The Everest-sized accreditations attained without a hitch, working together to make care accessible and safe through a pandemic, coordinating the practice sale, keeping a team engaged—these are the peaks and pinnacles I summitted on the climb. They were examples of *worth it* hard, or so I thought.

Did my past success resemble a battle because it was legitimately hard, or was it heavy because I gave to the wrong things? *Right* feels less punishing in this season. Change prompts contemplation about why and what needs to come. Was I ever meant to do what I did if it led to burnout despite notable achievement? Those years included lots of good, ample enough to keep me striving.

Either way, experience convinced me that what's deserving of effort and time must, without exception, feel difficult. Perhaps *hard* converts to *right* when the goal is yours. If so, there's a chance I long focused on the incorrect ridgeline and aspect of landscape.

From the top, the streams below are insignificant enough to dismiss and ignore. Small nothings. Yet, the sights within the valley, when you hang around longer than usual, expose those streams as the sustenance for the bold rivers, mapping a better route.

Those watercourses, be it rivers or streams, are the reading, the movement and what flows and grows from commitment, presence and rest. They're the refreshing splashes of possibility that dampen my legs as I cross the calmer sections of water, the serendipities in scenarios and selections. The streams of action, habit and thought form rivers of joy in the same way fallen tears in past rough waters shaped the valley.

Imagine the outcomes if I direct my efforts towards what's right for me. I'm familiar with *hard* and accustomed to doing *the work,* so stick close to the steady streams and see what comes.

Many of these big life queries and shifts make sense. The best discoveries are the hints not to go back, to avoid losing myself on top of another mountain. Sustain this renewed zest at a lower elevation for pleasant days ahead. *Good* doesn't need to be an all-consuming pursuit towards any peak. I'm on my way, strolling along the banks.

12 August 2024

Constructions of reality

The shift within is immense. Discomfort obliged more than change and awareness. Much more. In breaking, I discovered solutions, antidotes to self-destruction. While burnout stole a lot, it also limited the relentless advance of further damage, relieving me of my wobbling lone post with force. It put a full stop to mistreatment of myself, pushing me out of the way. Hence, burnout *can* be the counteragent to annihilation of my life, if handled with care.

There's peace in letting things fall away, while accepting that distress awoke me to something bigger. It allowed me to explore and construct an alternate reality. This represents a shift in me, to love where I am. The relief is an internal celebration of the grandest kind, a private fireworks display in my sky. I restore and renew as I rest on my blanket of calm in the open field beneath the twinkling gala of lights. I'm recalibrating, and the grass is indeed greener past the pain.

In this place, there's no expectation to withstand circumstances that others expect or prefer. I owe no explanations, and my next steps will follow this theme. I call it preservation, while contributing and achieving better than before. Technically, anything is possible if there are light shows in my sky.

Question of the day: Does rest detract from my power, and is this chapter of self-care lessening my impact? This period's providing, not taking. Roll with it, roll in this green, green grass!

Smiles replace palpitations as I unpack my amazement at where I am. My task is to shape and stack each handcrafted brick, one by one, to prosper as I rebuild with steady hands. Clay moulds and stacks in unique ways, with character, hardiness and versatility. Habits do too. I'm building a boundary around this greatness, foundations to resist the elements. Note: self-discovery and strength are best when malleable, yet robust.

I'm thankful for the realisations and skills that crisis exposed. To reshape what I assumed was fixed and predetermined is a welcome clay between my fingers. Burnout gave rise to an elevated and sustainable life, one I couldn't grasp, imagine or allow in the past.

Build on and take this chance at a softer reality long-term. This is your opportunity to complement what's already benefiting and stacking.

13 August 2024

It's all new

T he musings count. The reading, the exercise and early dark mornings, venturing into the forest and the strenuous work at the farm. Each empowers sublime time alone.

I'm not wanting for much; to meet each emotion with honesty and grace is sufficient. Consideration of my wants and needs is an upgrade. It's all new, and it's all nice.

Peace replaces the chaos of unhealthy high performance, while structure and discipline continue to serve. If applied in meaningful ways, these allies are also gurus of the recovery trade. Fabulous, considering I exude them in spades.

Unpacking my individuality, sensitivities and flaws helps me form a wholesome identity, a new and liberating one. My reactions are softening too. This flows as the natural outcome. I won't return to the person I had to be for everyone else; I closed that part of me.

I'm verbalising my spirit to those closest to me because it's difficult to contain. Peace hasn't been close by for a while, although it existed in the fun with the kids, throughout the pages read, on my yoga mat and amongst the simple things the entire time.

In no longer racing through the cool-downs of all aspects of life, I've found an aura of tranquillity, a swaddle of protective transformation that cocoons. For me, this is about as plausible as becoming besties with Wonder Woman. The encounters with knotty emotions, experiences, characters (not Wonder Woman) and coincidences guided me here. It all had to happen as it did.

Morning of 14 August 2024

Growth and magic happen in the details

When hope returns, a special magic follows. If this supernatural-like state gets any better, my white unicorn will appear soon, right on cue. The alternative explanation is that I'm already galloping through and towards the shimmering fairy lights on the edge of the meadow. My grateful attitude now requires little effort; it lifts naturally. Whimsical days. Details I would once rush over or miss in the busyness and strain bring deep happiness.

To declare I love my life because worry no longer consumes it is growth. Growth sandwiched between some enchanted, new, low-stress bread served with a side of calorie-free fries. Too good, more magic.

As this momentum builds in the right way, my direction is clear. Clear is right here. I've not experienced this magic before, but I'm shimmying towards the disposition of a genuine believer. My new trust in fate, along with lifestyle modifications, assembles a holistic existence. How exciting to discover that everything I needed I possessed all along. The difference is in what I notice, what I choose.

Is healing wizardry in human form? Could be.

Can romanticising recovery aid recovery? Yes!

Burnout handed me a broomstick, a mode of transportation out of the pot. Kind of dark, yet effective in helping one escape far, far away. The rewards of subtraction and restoration are reminders. Reminders of why I had to flee what I once tagged as acceptable.

I get it now; delusion personified is hope absent of alternative action, repeating what doesn't work and trusting others would do for me what I had to do for myself. I wished upon my delusive stars for improvement and change to appear like a rabbit from a hat. The rabbit didn't show, but heartache relayed that the magic and change both live within. Long there, waiting. Turns out, the magician responsible for transforming the trick was *me*.

Thanks to change, moments accumulate to form a radiant future picture, free from meaningless grind and full of this magical stuff. Burnout spared me, not from a dip in the cauldron, but from throwing my life away, from missing more of the boys growing up.

Sure, it's all self-indulgent, but it's developmental and hinges on my desire to stretch as I grow. It's tough to master anything life-changing, comebacks included, without a sprinkle of hedonism stirred into the work. I'm trusting my intentions and the magic are correct. Or at least enough to propel me onwards towards what my future needs to be. The brightness, which could well be the distant fairy lights, leaves me astonished, moved by the wonder. Canter on, white unicorn.

Afternoon of 14 August 2024

Burnout got me here

As I convert my handwritten journals, sadness blends with elation as I read over my experience. Typing these out might be an adventure in itself. I'm unsure where it will lead.

Astray in a one-dimensional wasteland of stress, my job demanded all I had, and I gave it. Desperate to make it work, my standard answer involved more ongoing sacrifice, despite certainty it was no longer the right place to be. My focus was on my obligation to others, to those I respected and supported. But in my effort to be my best, I erected a neon *Dump here* sign and welcomed and dealt with whatever arrived. My intention to be amiable, available and capable cost me a lot.

On this drizzly Wednesday afternoon, listening to the boys frolic with their friends in the street, I understand I was wrong. Not amiss to try, but incorrect to prioritise rubbish. Every day was bin day, but in reverse; the loads kept returning to me.

I moved fast while dealing with garbage for years. So many things. My role, two miscarriages, returning to the office with my breastfeeding pump in my back pocket too soon. Add in the multiple investment projects, buying, renovating, selling, moving, subdividing blocks of land and sanitising rental properties in the wake of tenants, navigating the cancellation of dreams, late-night cleaning and batch cooking, and tight handovers between opposing rosters in the car park in time for Steven to clock on for his next night shift. Our limited chances to connect beyond logistics, days, overtime and nights added to the strain, but we did it as everyone does.

I missed a lot while achieving a lot—another trade-off brimming with guilt and bewilderment. How did I interpret this as right, glamorising the delusion, dressing ridiculous volumes of responsibility in a pantsuit that communicated all was fine? I believed things were okay. We established a secure future, owned the tough decisions and saluted our correct and brave moves. One project led into the other, and everything overlapped. That's life.

My regret, my biggest one, is the time I missed with Jackson and Leo when they were young. My heart tells me I'm overthinking it. They're carefree kids, surrounded by a village of grandparents, plus us. Steven more than earned his title of Best Dad. They had more quality time with their dad than most kids could dream of—the bright side of my absence. I convinced myself I was serving us, serving them, given the comparable income my efforts contributed. Wrong again. Time is money, but time is also freedom, and I had none.

Did everything lead me here, and am I alright with that? I am. There's a reason for each detour, triumph and difficulty. I now inhale the freshness that follows the rain. Simple pleasures and rights, like being close by as the boys drift off to sleep—I'm here for them. We chat, and I'm home for their requests: "Mum, lie with me in my bed and tuck me in."

Witnessing the wildlife and the way the dusk sunlight radiates greenery before it disappears for the day; taking moments to breathe and eat lunch—these things are now in my life because I burnt out. Peace wouldn't have traction today had I not suffered while maintaining a skip bin on my desk/kerb for others to fill at their will. I approved distress and overload. I wasn't expecting immediate satisfaction post removal of all I thought I had to deal with, and now I won't ever again wait to exit a situation that's unreasonable. Thanks to the affliction that compelled me to seize essential change, I reclaimed what matters. Burnout got me here.

All of this was in my head today

My aspirational future self—who would she be, how would she look, what might she say if she were sitting here with me?

A refined older woman enters my mind. Dressed in casual black linen pants, she's her own library category of calm. Her eyes sit behind glasses, and her flowing grey hair brushes the top of her waist. Contentment encompasses her, a comforting glow.

She's smiling as she reads, learning for enjoyment's sake. She exudes resilience, a presence. There's something classic and grounding in her confidence. This lady's wrinkles share the storylines of her life. The gathering of her smile creases conveys a narrative of living well, despite adversities. The release from chronic stress years ago erased pain and offered wisdom many are not fortunate to find.

There's a bookshelf, housing books and memories with her husband and children, behind where she sits. The people in the pictures are my boys; she is really me at a future point in time.

Her bookshelf is full. My book collection has expanded, like her life, to fill the large floor-to-ceiling wall of printed riches. To the right of her shoulder sits a light-coloured hardcover book embossed with my name. I can't make out the title, but my imagination assumes it alludes to repair. Could it be these writings, my rough compilations of healing, the ones I'm composing now?

Hopefully, I'm becoming her, but for now, I'm becoming me, and that's enough.

She didn't speak, but if she had a message, it would be: *Go on as you are. Listen and learn all you can. Focus on what's essential. Lean into the small moments; they will merge to comprise your great life. This will all work out. It already has.*

My daydream about my future makes all sorts of sense. Plus, I now have an excuse for why nonfiction books fill my home. I'm preparing for my full-height bookcase one day soon. My books are my solace, valued possessions that expand motivation with each verse. Daily reading remains my recreation of choice. Books gift courage, safety nets and strategies; they move me through change. Reading affords positivity, even amid the workloads and busier years.

Baseline peace mode is my preferred, adored state. Productivity here is like paddling through a serene lake with controlled and deliberate strokes. I'm in one place at a time, a decadent promotion and an integral piece of the recuperation puzzle. Pretty simple, just no longer hidden in plain sight.

Hence, I now detect the cherry-red bush berries amongst the ferns on my way to the creek, the trickle of water and the birds welcoming me. Sometimes I take a book, but often only the dogs. Other visits are all about drawing in the earthy scent of the mud that paints the forest floor and my gumboots, or the fluttering butterflies in their floaty elegance meandering on by. Nature reciprocates, on repeat. Thankful to live here, and to now have more time here.

Right now is my healthier place; stay, maintain this. Burnout often precedes a breakthrough. This is that. There are lessons in reflection, in walking away to walk forward, renewed. I listened, changed, and I'm better off.

From distress to calm seemed a quick transition, though it wasn't. I'm fortifying because I'm working on it every day. Some days, that work involves consolidating my resume ahead of who knows what's next while appreciating the reminders of all I achieved. I blocked it out courtesy of my emotions about deserting who I thought I was, the person I built. I didn't fail; I achieved until I couldn't anymore.

I didn't expect to be ready to stomach anything career-related for months, but if what I select next is tiny in comparison, thinking about it is less scary. There's no rush to return; however, I need to face my fears about how work fits into my future. It too is part of healing and moving on.

Regardless of this precious existence I'm crafting, droplets of doubt and worry keep me cautious. Do I trust myself to protect it? I can write for days about choosing less long-term, but can I actually do it? Will I dive straight back into people-pleasing by honest mistake? Can I ignore larger roles with my name on them? Am I ready for anything at all? This period of no set plans is a beautiful thing, but sometimes a source of insecurity and slight concern.

To confirm I'm serious about this flexible, self-serving approach, at some point, I'll have to give it a go. Not sure how yet. I might need to develop some criteria for returning to work to settle my nerves. Sit with this. Progress equals taking steps towards her, my future self, while weaving my professional abilities into a situation that provides purpose, space and productivity. In the rewrite of my story, I have bandwidth to think, a chance to become.

17 August 2024

Criteria

Taking notes as I try something out is today's attempt at not turning back towards burnout. Insurance, if anything, and a means to recall my body's immediate replies.

Leadership position? No way! *Quick click to the next ad.*

Senior receptionist at a busy practice. Nope, *click.*

Manage a large team. Instant queasiness, not again in this lifetime, *quick click.*

Nine-day fortnight practice management role. Ha ha, that doesn't work. I can't. *Click.*

Basic administrator. Too basic, boring, *click.*

Advance the division. Done that, and it involves managing people, which makes anxiety return, so no, *click.*

Oversee a ten-doctor practice welcoming busloads of patients with potential for increasing responsibility. Not this time; my nerves say no more limitless responsibility. *Click.*

Government department temp contract. It'd be difficult to get, *click.*

Casual hospital administration. No reaction, and the hours would be tricky, *click.*

Experienced medical administrator for a job-share position in a solo specialist practice, three days per week, close to home. This could fit, *save.*

Fascinating exercise, clicking through job adverts and observing my initial impressions and visceral reactions. An intuition stress test where gut feelings reveal plenty. Listening is how I'll know. My urge to move straight past everything that sparks instant tightness—that's my answer. This is how I'll build trust in my ability to make the right decision. It's wishy-washy, but as per my commitment to change, I'll go with the opposite of my usual approach.

Yesterday's idea of having a few guidelines might be okay. Intuition and criteria—such a strange match. At least it's more measured than emotions alone and removed enough from my standard meticulous aim-high style. Record a few ideas and see where it leads.

Possible criteria for ensuring I return to the workforce as a person, not a workhorse:

One: There's zero time-pressure to return. But if something's a good fit, there's no requirement to wait either, provided it's not more than four days per week. Months of savings back me up. However, a small opportunity would supplement an extended stay in this new life.

Two: As a means of self-protection, embrace an earnings cap. It will rule out everything I do not need. Jobs paying less equal lower stress and more of this life. Play small across the board. Strange and conflicting, going backwards on purpose, but trust the process (and myself). Any inkling of dread, or if large fancy jobs appeal, stop. The safest word is *no*. If a pleasant, stepped-down option shows up, explore that.

Three: Observe what relays back. Have faith in the gut-feeling test. Don't move ahead until satisfying this. It means prioritising my needs over what I can do for others while discarding my old classification of success, for real. Intuition must overshadow professional pride.

Four: If anything gets through the above, imagine what the future would look like if that role entered the mix—how would it affect this reality I worked to achieve. If it still sits right, reach out. Detach and listen to the silence or the reply. They'll be as telling as each other if I flow with fate.

Five: If a reply comes, go through this entire list again prior to committing to an interview or anything resembling a next step. Still a *yes?* If so, try it in action.

These are rough, repetitive perimeters, but it's a start—and way more productive than worrying about what-ifs. Consider applying for that little job saved today, the one that sounds too good to be true. At least see how it fares against the above. Go from there.

18 August 2024

Moving through

The unknowns ahead now motivate, not scare. This happens when the monsters of worry move on. Open windows and a limitless life—it's different. This headspace carries a sense of delight, like the aroma of fresh-cut flowers and crisp linens their first night on the bed. Once found, there's no going back. No job can erase it.

To move through this experience on my own terms is my greatest contribution to self. I create the destination, my second chance. The choice to end my dedication to formidable anxiety is self-care rebalancing step one of 101.

This morning, it looks like writing by the creek. The old arched gate leading down, made from repurposed timber and decorated with a spreading layer of fine moss, could easily work as a reference for a fairy door to another realm in one of Pixar's vivid animation movies. This gate marks the entrance to a concealed garden of sorts and more of all that's encased by green peace.

Our gate and private garden stand for a lot: the entry to a captivating way through. Like the moss, happiness envelops me whenever I approach and open the gate. There's symbolism in what it represents—escapism and a gentler certainty in a familiar and special place, on my doorstep. Beyond its potential for cinema screens, my fairy gate grants access to somewhere lifted. My offering to the fairies and the forest is gratitude.

Personal evolution means I'm open to things once out of focus or comprehension, even fairies, so it seems. A successful day is one where I'm at ease, not consumed by tension and the unessential. Burnout-level busy left room for nothing except the next task, and so on. Far from living, closer to plotting one's own undoing. I almost tripped too far through the wrong gate.

On the flip side, fulfilment favours the brave and revolves around what feeds the roots of growth. I won't accept a future that pressurises a choice between wellbeing and productivity. I'll apply for the job I saved yesterday. This is me trusting as I release: *three, two, one, go*. The fibres of being, the ones I collected by hand and hard work along the way, combine to strengthen my journey over the pass.

What appears created and formed by chance is by precise design. The creek bed, littered with fallen branches and trees from past storms, reinforces my new *according to plan* narrative. Over time, the water flow gathered and positioned tiny elements into a formation vital for the water to move in the ideal direction. Each occurrence serves as a preparation for the next. Everything's in place. The sticks, rocks and leaves overlap to form something else. They impart a story of all that came before, while shaping what's predetermined to follow. Nature knows. Pay attention.

I am! The whipbirds' morning singing shift begins, drawing me away from the page. Glancing up, I'm met with more reminders of why I'm here. Noticing the sunlight seeping through the canopy signals I'm aware of my many fortunes already present and lasting. They surrounded me the whole time, but I was spiritually shut down.

19 August 2024

What feels right is right

S teven and I are working at the farm again today. After drenching our hands in sanitiser, we drink hot flask tea on the house plateau looking down the mountain.

Life in one of the most diverse and stimulating places on the planet feels healthy and right. Days here honour the responsibility Rob handed us many months ago. *We're doing it, Rob, paying homage to your wishes, keeping the farm in the family.*

Rob's memory lives on as we strive to restore the place, as long as it takes. The rugged complexity up here reminds me of him. Rob walked his talk and lived his way, both strong and stoic. I tell him I care each time I wander up the track, past his weathered Akubra resting on the black rock below the mango tree. Singapore daisy, the prettiest of weeds, decorates his spot.

The farm and Rob's trust in us further propagate my appreciation of nature and the land. The enormity and intricacy of land and weed management educate us all. As a result, my aspirations run deeper and wider. Things mean more across all life ecosystems. The waterfalls feed the streams as much as the rainforest creates air.

Gazing over the range, I take in the towering ancient pine that adds dimension to the expansive view. As a selected caretaker of the mountain, I've inherited opportunities and challenges to fill a lifetime. From managing one wilderness to another, I prefer the upkeep that comes with this one, despite harder and larger. Stretching out, spent and able, I understand why Rob adored it here. In the quietude is education, and in nature lives purpose.

As each day passes, I'm liking the person I'm becoming a little more. I'm improving my ability to let the echoes of my past set with the sun as the person who comes through for everyone drifts downstream. The strange extra expanse here by the tree, and in me, allows me to sip rather than gulp my tea. These days, Steven and I even spend time together!

"Do you want more tea, babe, before we keep going?" I ask.

"I'm good, thanks," he says, mid-kelpie-belly pat with one hand and wiping the fine layer of dirt covering his face with the other.

Moving ahead like this assures a future of expanding joy. There's capacity for more. Joy, I mean, not tea.

20 August 2024

Six weeks to here

Change is preferable to suffering; that's a statement of fact. I'm six weeks into my tour of personal safety. Six weeks since I strayed from the pack. My aim is to embrace the days of my one-woman expedition. I'm maintaining a pace but also resting as if it's the ultimate retreat-style vacation.

Quite the experience so far, exploring my emotions while marvelling at the abundant wildlife here in our nature-filled backyard. Six full weeks of relishing the kids, my environment and all things green close to and around home. The sweetness in the air, like boronias after rain, complements the pleasing changes unfolding within me. Six weeks I would live on repeat if I could, and maybe I will!

Another fact: change is the answer to my troubles.

More truth: the elevated cliff road I took to escalating burnout was a crazy, mind and spirit-breaking way of living. I could only navigate the edge of danger so many times before the ground crumbled or the tyres lost tread. Dead ends, warnings and loud bangs presented for valid reasons. In passing the *Unsafe to proceed* signs lining the side of the road, my progress was limited to filling potholes to motor on. Headlights dimmed, fading into the dark and winding abyss.

Reality: I'm free to choose, experiment and discover. I can put things out there and see what returns. Turns out, rock bottom morphed into an unexpected golden ticket. An advantage in creating a desirable life. I earned the lifetime perks included with my pass. Everything's an impressive uplift.

One of the best findings: transparent water with a white sand bottom best portrays my thinking. It's clear. My colour has also returned, and time is no longer erased by worry but directed towards what's real. This warmth in my soul means I'm in the right place; I'm with my family.

I'll avoid any situation that demands I go all-in on another trip up the cliff road. Boundaries will remain, and my new vested interest in wellbeing will have no end. As the small things become my key things, some clichés—beauty in simplicity and subtract to gain, for example—are too vital to ignore. The work to get here was worthwhile. It's all worthwhile.

I'm sure because distance dispels the doubts I had about identity. My needless concerns were mere pieces of the larger mystery, fragments of the rewarding unknown. In gathering experiences and days as myself, I know what I like, need and give. My character, my worth, is connected to how I feel each day, not the tasks I complete. Work and quality remain central to how I operate, but harmony now dominates over hustle. I'm a high achiever who chose life. This makes me strong. And, to top it all, I'm smiling about who I am and the person I'm continuing to meet.

Re-entry

This existence will continue indefinitely in some form. I'll need to re-enter the work world soon, although this return to reality will be smooth with less to worry about. With change comes experience, and with experience comes ease. The pastures are ready to cushion me.

I might return to an office sooner than planned. Amid yesterday's efforts stripping the walls of the farm shack back to hardwood frames, a reply arrived inviting me to interview for the part-time mid-level role I found the fortitude to apply for a few days ago.

Dusty work gloves removed and my developing intuition sensors on high alert, reading the email cultivated more calm. A great start.

The interview's tomorrow, sooner than expected, but it could be the right re-entry.

I'm eager to entertain less, to honour my promise of lasting change. The purpose of my surrender was to arrive and settle somewhere new. The discoveries I made along the way confirm my efforts long orbited the wrong sun. Not anymore. In recent weeks, I floated alone through star-filled skies in preparation to rejoin people (but not too many people) with greater self-interest than before. And now, this opportunity arises with a welcome that's too confirmatory to ignore.

Either way, I get to choose, and I have to trust myself to choose—an enormous responsibility considering what I selected and tolerated in the past. Leave my self-image afloat in space so I can take wise next steps. A lesser position equates to more of this life and the actualisation of my allegiance to change. It's the first test of follow-through and where best to invest.

As my life expands, pleasing constellations of questions and truths illuminate my airspace. Keep looking up. No doubt, what appears will align. Don't disregard what presents with little effort. That's where you need to land this time. There's sense amongst the sequences of feelings and stars.

23 August 2024

What comes to me

Okay, self-imposed demotions are where it's at!

I got the job. It's so right that I accepted on the spot. Hopefully, this is a good thing. Either way, this is me embracing change and life in all areas.

Today's experience spelled out as a giant and immediate *yes*. The interview flowed more like a reunion between friends. Natural, comfortable, meant to be, but importantly, I was me. My easygoing and honest articulation was impressive enough to resonate. I too met my upgraded self in that room today.

The role's so small in comparison to my last position, which is soothing in its own right. No promises or big asks, and there's no need because it's straightforward, *just* a job.

This intersection of glad and proud places a green tick in my *choose differently next time* box. Touch wood, I found it, my entry point to a counterbalanced coexistence between work and life. I call this part *more change and ongoing revival.*

26 August 2024

Mastering myself

I achieved a level of professional mastery. I broke for the sake of it. But self-mastery—that's another region of my internal world. This experience transfers me there, to the long-lost land of becoming an expert on oneself. It's a bonus this is possible here amongst the estate of home. My mind ventures far and wide while I remain in place.

In feeling safe, I'm mastering the fluctuations between the octaves of my emotions and states, honing my ability to regulate back to base. I'm deliberate about getting out of my own way: many thanks, burnout. The steady and building anticipation greeting me at the dawn of each day—that's me getting acquainted with my soul. Who is this person embracing the alarm clock in the early hours with glee?

I'm achieving separation from worry (mostly) and other feats. I'm healing because I removed the stress-inducing cause, but the chain reaction of change aids and adds to the positive force. Intuition is my companion and alarm, a protective offsider. As in, trust your alarms from this day forward and trust them early. Not like last time. Don't stay if your body instructs you to run. Useful advice ahead of what's next.

Tomorrow's the day before a new stage begins. This time, my task isn't to master a job, but to sustain this lighter life while complementing it with some work. I welcome the test. The past weeks packed with choice and experiences delivered me here, to this place of calm. My active pause, the emotional aria of my life, my moving serenade to self in my amphitheatre for one, in my heart.

As I step closer to mastering myself, I choose and maintain what's important. My family, the admiration that wakes me each morning, spirituality, habit-enhancing self-care, routine and ritual. These *real* breaks will exist in the future too, and I'll remain available for the boys. Self-discovery is what I imagine walking the arcs of rainbows would be like while wrapping my mind around what I want. I'm creating it with every step, each word, book and bedtime story shared. I'm becoming her, the lady with the long silver hair, the version of me who picks the flowers and stares at the shape of the moon. I am conscious. In attention is joy. While mastering me, I'm mastering being here, now.

27 August 2024

The day I saw the seasons change

The springtime aromas arrived a few days early. Wild jasmine lines the border fence of home. Rustic hedges of blooms extend for metres down both sides. These little white florets are the spring boundaries framing my space and perfuming the house with renewal.

The season's changing, and for the first time, I'm witnessing the shifts in the air, the warmer presence of daylight and the splash of the kids jumping in for the first swim. We're transitioning to spring, but the walls of jasmine signal it's already here.

The blooming new beginnings making my day do so with serendipitous alignment, on the eve of my next season. Ahead of a fresh start tomorrow, my nurturing winter of recovery also draws to a partial close. The season too is ready to change, adapt, blossom and bloom.

This real-time sensory gift confirms *everything* will soon flower. Today will stay with me. The scent of spring's first jasmine is the most fitting metaphor for the way I'm living and growing.

Like the borders of wildflowers, my upcoming season will show me the way. I did this, chose it, released fear and redeemed my sanity. The winter was anything but dormant. It prepared me for the spring.

To bloom is to be open. I'm open and turning towards the sun. The gratitude is immeasurable, as is the beauty of the spring fence lines.

Here for a reason

Rise and shine, next chapter. Hello, more healing and well done you. Is relaxed/exhilarated/assured even a thing? Today it is. Don't forget this morning, this feeling. Note it down.

Sensing my gusto as I put the finishing touches on school lunches, Steven, coffee in hand, planted a kiss on my cheek. "Exciting day for you, babe."

"Yeah, first day in a position I'd usually be the one hiring someone for. Less is right—weird but right."

"It sounds perfect." The comfort of his large hand resting on my back as I washed the chopping board, gazing out the kitchen window at the yard, was complete approval. Phew, he's pleased and relieved too. I'll keep our exchange close as I embark on this beautiful day.

My light-hearted mood this morning says it all, and the reassuring chimes of the bells of relief ring loud and true. I'm doing it, as promised. I'm choosing new truths and building on the past months in a serving way.

My old all-or-nothing life in one arena is done, finished. Today I'm joining a team of four (including me), no longer assuming responsibility for a classroom-size cohort, everything and more. This role offers job share, backup and the indulgence of working alone. More solitude? Yes, please. If job heaven exists for the recently burnt out, I'm entering it.

Although unfamiliar, committing to a step down in responsibility is me advocating for myself and manifesting my motivational brief from June, the one where sure things mattered and uncertainty incited fear. Here in August 2024, I'm self-help in action, and self-help delivers the goods.

I'll explore my lingering anxieties in relation to how my ego and bank account are affected by my smaller life down the line as needed. Plenty more to come, I'm sure. But in the meantime, and so doubt can't talk me out of it, I'm trying genuine change on for size. Today is the day. Besides, burnout's left me little choice but to afford myself the luxuries and treatment I grant everyone else. That's what this is—the empath within showing up for me. Anyhow, I'm certain I arrived here on purpose and sense that it's all part of some larger plan. I'll write more later, after work.

Winning

Day two of my new work situation. It's unlike my classification of *work*, in a refreshing dip-in-the-ocean way. So far, this role fits the one-thing-at-a-time, done-well ethos I'm adopting across my life. Superbly. Perhaps this was the answer the whole time, my move from manager of much and many to medical secretary for one.

The rooms are small and welcoming, with seating in understated pastel tones. I'll heal just spending time there. Serenity lingers throughout. Tucked away from the bustle of the attached hospital and any iteration of chaotic demand, I hear… quiet, apart from the occasional phone call. Even the phone rings with a sweet tune, a single line at a time. My open but shielded desk renders Perspex infection-control spit-screens unnecessary. A tenth of the patients per hour means more air.

And the view! The wall of windows framing the skyline and the budding jacaranda tree in the park replaces my previous porthole view to the outside that I failed to discern. That's on me. My unlikely pivot aligns with my journey from stress to seas of greater calm, also known as specialist medical practice. My role's minimalistic, administrative and revolves around nurturing new life in more ways than one. Funny that. I traded broad-scale practice for supporting the medicine of newborns and new mums.

Despite the switch, working with inspiring and caring doctors continues. Old-school, down-to-earth, patient-centred dedication lives here too, prompting fond memories of the past doctor crew I was fortunate to assist.

From what I can tell, this position is all I imagined less *could* bring. I found my spot, or at least another confirmation of the virtue in change. We located each other, Utopia and me. Today's more proof that a correct option exists.

All those years, I was too strait-laced to mull over anything intuitive, unless it guaranteed an outcome or logical step up. I took a lot of those. But hey, people can be dumb. I raise my hand.

Regardless of my mistakes, and in some ways because of them, I gained clarity over these past months. More (clarity) came today via Jackson's tight squeeze welcoming me home. "Mum, it's not even dark yet and you're home early again, like you promised. I like this job better." Squeezing me a little longer than usual and gifting a nod, he headed back out to play.

"Thank you, Universe," I uttered under my breath while placing my bag down in the daylight hours of my new normal Thursday afternoon. Gratitude is appropriate because during recent bedtime chats both boys confided worries about my return to work.

Over the past couple of weeks, when I broached the prospect, Leo's standard comment from his plush toy-laden comfy kingdom on the top bunk was without fail some version of a hard no. "Not yet. Stay with us longer, Mum," he'd say. "You've only been home for a little while."

Jackson's interest was twofold. For the first time in his life, he agreed with Leo, but he was also concerned about time. "Yeah, agree. Anyway, will you be home late? What time? Before dinner?"

"This will be different," I told them each time. "I'll be here with you most days and back early, promise."

Provide the assurances they need, stay honest, clear and consistent in my replies so they trust I'll be around. This was me delivering on my word to them. I must, because their awareness is my reminder that the only title they care about is my headline as their mum.

My recurring thoughts today:

Winning.

Seek and you shall receive.

Change is worth it.

I get to be a mum.

They need and love me as much as I love them.

Trust that you can do this; you already are.

Use the momentum.

The balance is real.

Everything led here

I catch myself smiling in moments all the time. Outwardly and within, at all things great and small. I call them self-smiles, these reactions to my appealing reality.

Brief and light, the season's easy-to-miss sun showers deposit a lasting luminosity on both cheeks and leaves. I can now exhale as I release the past and move towards more of this, towards living. Spring is yet to begin, but the emotional quantities of quality arrived early.

In gathering the profits of labour and change from the foundational beds where I once planted seeds, I'm the producer of my harvests and happiness. As in, I'm toiling with all I have for a life that's lighter on my spirit and generous to my soul. I didn't expect these emotions. I'm long familiar with the opposite end of the spectrum, but an inquisitive stranger here. The seedling menu offered this option all along.

Despite some difficult turns, my past shaped my resilience, one completed list and challenge at a time. Ironically, it also got me here.

As the clouds clear, the hard times fade into distant but necessary memories. I'm receiving regular recalls of why I had to experience the extremes. Everything, although testing, led me somewhere nicer. To this place where endurance swaps out for enjoyment, where choice is a given and managing and meeting everyone's needs is no longer my thing. This lets me be someone exceptional for the closest few, to sort and nurture only our own little crop. My everything-to-everyone era missed the point—that seedlings need a fine-tuned combination of *basics* to grow. There's room for more. There's time for what's real. Muted environments, projects, scope to process and reap the benefits and origins of each smile.

This stage brings it all together—the hamper of harvested goods, the highs and lows, the truths that helped me arrive and make some sense of past discomforts. Since removing my perfectionist gloves, the satisfying textures of the moist, fertile and adaptive soil give meaning and dimension. The essentials give meaning and dimension.

For years, I was graceful under pressure. People told me so. But I worked my way up to torn and unwell, willing to serve and assume the responsibilities of a small nation if asked. Although I hold slight uneasiness about letting so much go, I'm not reducing my standards or goals. I'm raising them. Receptivity has no ceiling.

I deserve fun and spontaneous smiles alongside work. Redesign a livable life, one where I gain. The layered stories are the heartfelt ones because they are real, like the smiles.

Before bed on 30 August 2024

Burnout so far

Reading more about burnout helps me process the experience, which so far has gone like this…

The lead-up, or my life before

As part of my important job, I took on more and more and more. Busy looked elegant on me. I'm tall, so I carried it well. People-pleasing satisfied something within; my ambition, eagerness and willingness to give more were unwavering. Driven to strive harder and longer whenever required, everything returned a yes (except my needs). Required equalled always because someone somewhere could end up disappointed if I said no. The catch—*I* didn't count as a someone.

I worked with the best intentions, but day after day the demands consumed the hours in the wrong ways. The polite *please come back later* request I pasted to my door at the height of my frustration proved a lousy thin paper shield for the reams of interruptions.

Despite feeling used up, I was still so nice. My dedication unlocked higher acclaim, and without a doubt, more work. My workload shared similarities with those monotonous, charged ballads with no end. I delivered a lot, longing for it to stop.

Being obsessively available, and hence in no way free, was counterintuitive. I embodied reliability and neglected my needs; how noble of me. As a skilled giver and glorified doormat, I suppressed my needs so the areas I entered functioned well. My panicked thoughts of change added to my lists. Too painful to touch. Self-care seemed trivial, and my longing to scream while punching a wall visited often; my exhaustion prevented me from acting on either.

Each request crippled hope more. Even my coffee tasted sour by the time I got to my cold and curdled cup. Resentment for the position that had become my life coexisted with love and hate for all that I strived for.

Of course I worked extra; everyone has tough periods. That's what it was. Another one. I lied about coping, a preservation of sorts, until it wasn't. Sacrificing everything else hurt, and Steven and the boys copped some version of *I can't, I'm sorry,* and *I have to work* more often than the dogs barked.

I was functional but struggling, if dragging my essence along the floor passes as functional. My life took a back seat. Right to the far edge of the seven-seater SUV's back row.

Breaking point

Shoving aside the mounting symptoms of breakdown allowed me to get on with the task, until one day I became the task. My repeating question: What's the use? No effort will ever be enough.

I missed my family. Hello, guilt.

Head in my hands, I wished everyone would leave me alone to think, just long enough to rescue myself. Distress and uncertainty came to stay. I was unsure how I'd summon the strength to stand again tomorrow and each day beyond that.

The prickly numbness and stress told me something was incorrect. Family and friends expressed concern too (I cried for aid and advice at some stage).

Exhausted but wired and unable to sleep, it kept getting worse. Unwell, with an acute awareness of the pace I had to keep, I cared as greatly as I ached. My depletion and desperation led to admission, although it could have also been my intensifying pain.

With acknowledgement entered thoughts of options, change and restorative action. *What if?* Impressions, perspectives and questions churned in muddled loops. I asked for help, understanding that no one would arrive. Despite much discussion and goodwill, the duties kept multiplying. Time to help myself.

Change

Thankfully, adrenaline kicked in, enough to confirm and commit to my exit. I worked towards removing the stressor (and me). Resignation was the gift burnout selected. I am, as I have noted, lucky.

To facilitate a smooth release, I gave one last heave, doing the right thing by everyone else, including me this time.

Pride intact, I walked away without a plan other than fantasies about sleep. I smiled for real as I waved my office goodbye, recalling the brighter years before breakdown joined my team. I detached in every way, exiting all aspects of my professional life, trusting things would be okay as I held Steven and the boys close.

Next, I collapsed onto a king-sized pillow of repose, into a different life. I slept and then celebrated the freedom that came with my new beginning, unaware it was also a sort of becoming.

The reassuring intermission after change

I healed as I rested. My work became personal work. I focused on cultivating more of what served—sincere and concentrated wellness from the bottom of my heart. Self-love entered the room. Choice, strength and positivity returned too. Uncertainty delivered unexpected surprises, strengthening my faith in the leap.

I released as I explored, and my introspection morphed into a rejuvenating personal evolution.

Initial ideas about my new reality developed into a breathtaking, understated existence—I thanked the Universe every day.

Lessons so far

My burnout was unlikely to resolve on its own. It was worth a try, ignoring and pushing on while willing my situation to improve. However, big changes, culminating from many smaller ones, have proved to be my ideal intervention to date.

Some scenarios are harsh, no matter the outlay, superficial tweaks and willing acceptance. Preparation and hunkering down is often a wise strategy, but sometimes this falls short. In my case, it was best that I moved on. After all, the nature of a beast is to be the biggest and best it can be. Plus, it was beyond difficult to withstand burnout's unrelenting impact without reprieve. Chief Everything Officer (CEO) is the promotion achieved by diligent and quick-thinking care bears like me. I excelled but cared so much I brought myself to ruin while remaining compassionate and considerate—a rare skill that comes at a price.

Because of burnout, my boundaries now matter. Obvious ones that articulate to passersby that this is my line, the way white picket fences or the grand brick pillar variety serve a purpose beyond aesthetics and facade. As per the quaint fence, the one by the frangipani wrapped in passionfruit vine, I could have afforded my attention to *any* sort of boundary sooner.

As we forever reminded the boys when they were little, if you need to go, go early. For me, the takeaway from burnout is similar, although deeper, and has nothing to do with not peeing my pants. I waited and willed my busting urge for comfort to go away. But relief requires action, and action doesn't action itself. Reaching breaking point was the epitome of a message from above. It pays to listen. The rest I'm figuring out.

Self-selection

This pleasing life is less about seeking or extracting alluring wins than it is about cultivating them from within, because a reality that doesn't serve, harms.

Thankfully, misplacement offers magnificent potential, spurring construction of stunning alternatives, not dissimilar to the life cycle of saltwater pearls. Organic and created by a creature as the result of a mistake entering a shell, pearls are an inspiring example of natural beauty forming from things being out of place.

The irritant, what doesn't belong—it could even be a fragment from the shell itself (hello, burnout)—activates a defence mechanism within the mollusc. Sounds familiar. At the least, a pretty parallel.

It gets better. The protective substance triggered by the irritant encapsulates and coats the foreign entity, layer by layer, until the accumulated coatings transform into a pearl. That's what I'm doing here, if coating something with new actions and perspectives, and gleaning meaning and reason from nature counts. For so long, I saw my situation as my big mistake. However, the hardships prompted an unexpected ability to make my own pearls. Records show I'm not too bad at dealing with irritants, so to speak. So, if burnout is the agitation that penetrated my life, change layers the transformational glaze for pure, valuable outcomes (the gems and jewels).

It doesn't end there, though, for the pearl or me. A pearl's lustre, how it reflects light, allows pearls by molluscs in saltwater to glow from within. Cultured varieties lack this quality. Apt, as the water I immersed myself in was, by my definition, harsh and salty. I viewed that as unfortunate luck, but perspective and distance alter a lot. Also, real pearls are a little gritty; the blemishes and imperfections confirm their authenticity. Encouraging. How the days and weeks feel holds greater weight and radiance than anything else. They're sitting well, organic and correct. My readiness to defend my environment and build protections against past triggers produces pearls for days. It seems that thoughtful overlays of positive activity are prerequisites for both intention and nature to fall into place, for nourishing and shielding progress to compound and shine with a pearly sheen.

Amazing to discover that success is possible without forfeiting every morsel of my needs. Plus, the products of effort and change provide reassurance to continue exploring the salty waters. I love that, because I located solutions and my sense of direction when I selected to work on my self-made string of pearls.

Part Four

Sustained Metamorphosis

1 September 2024

Investments in peace

I woke early to be in the garden and to welcome spring. My meditation attempt was short-lived, thanks to the alluring vista of green extending down beyond the forest, tempting me to peek. I sat, all senses smiling, absorbed by the enchanting sanctuary before me—meditation.

Presence is power, presence is peace. It all goes together. This dreamlike life scape will live on as long as I invest in it. Investments of self towards peace.

Throughout my recent emotional and spiritual inquisitiveness, I stumbled upon a place where I'll stay. The place is a headspace, vivid and surreal. I didn't envision this alternative other side. If my mindset were a physical place, it's our home and garden amalgamated with a secluded log chalet by a lake in a village beneath the Swiss Alps. It is fresh alpine air mixed with a hearty meal simmering on the wood stove, the whiff of smoke from embers, dewy grass and flowers frequented by dragonflies and bees. The vision is real; it's where I am.

To comprehend awe and such daydreams is as vital an asset as learning to walk or read. This is where I'll be, listening and collecting more inner capital to sustain my metamorphosis.

Picturesque villages and transformations aside, am I ignorant to think it will all be okay, choosing to earn less than what I did previously? The uncertainty stokes the coals of ambitious belief, handing me a chance to test, try and trust the whispers that tell me the unexpected and rewarding breaks in the clouds will continue to unfold. Instinct counts. It takes the edge off doubt and fear. Don't stop listening now. Don't step backward. Add more colour to your wings.

I walked the path that built a bank balance at the expense of everything else. This season and what's ahead are not that. To exchange dollars for time and tranquillity—isn't this what humanity strives for, anyway?

Yes after yes, my heart warms as I experience the pursuit, endeavour and destination in each day. I had time to help my neighbours this weekend. Giving without forgoing everything and all is what full lives are about. Allow life to be forever that. Sustain, hold on to and nurture the equilibrium you're fostering. It's the right choice, waking up and investing in yourself. The exciting part is getting to know your abilities, some of which you haven't even met yet.

3 September 2024

Gains

The discomfort in my past is minor compared to what others face. Insignificant in the scheme of things, but a lesson up close. I enjoyed being the person people relied on for the answers and the approach. The pressure motivated me to excel. But, to live for work, regardless of opportunity or capability, ate away at me.

As a workaholic I found it difficult not to work. Committed, effective, unhealthy, relentless, obsessed. That was me, too. My vice was work. The workaholic gets (or finds) more… work, sacrificing for a deadline, a moving finish line. I received no reprieve unless I could toil away. My responsibilities became both the enemy and a remedy, both consuming and placating while helping me get lost.

For a perfectionist addicted to work (a destructive biohazard to self), whatever's kept up high in the air falls with weight, eventually.

Time, grit and experience built my career, and what I thought was a life, while overthinking, overdelivering and ignoring sensible limits made me sick. The hard way was my escape from my multitasking pedestal. Burnout was my hard way. With nothing but more to-dos left, change had to be my boldest next move, so I chose that. I put some things down. Different, challenging, eye-opening, life-affirming. My environment had to change too, for an improved likelihood of success. I actioned that as well. To my advantage, full commitment is a characteristic of the workaholic personality. From office to outside and smothering four walls to vast semi-rural timberlands, I commissioned myself for a new piece of work. Healing.

Clarity hits with a similar thud to all the dropping crap that I once ran to keep elevated. Awareness landed with impact as I walked away on that day back in July. Awareness that I'm free when I release myself. I recover as I change and change as I recover. I get to choose what to sustain, and each shift aligns many gains.

Today consisted of a lovely morning with the kids, a productive workday, a brisk walk along the bush tracks and an uneventful weeknight at home, together. Dull, bordering on vanilla for some, but not to me.

Hi, I'm Hayley, once a workaholic, today not so much. Dedicated but practising putting at least one item down before picking anything else up. What follows the moment you drop handfuls of responsibility on the grass deserves greater attention than perfecting the self-perpetuating juggling skills of the overworked middle class. Sitting on the grass, palms empty, resembles sunbaking, but it's more than that. This is me gaining.

The race is over

I'm going to maintain that uttering "good morning" to my trusty espresso machine passes as reasonable.

The birds stir, but it's still dark; the morning hasn't quite begun. Soon it will, and I too will welcome the first light, the birds' chirping. Every morning, a unique energy unfolds as my coffee complements solitude and growth. Each action combines to create a double-shot infusion of anticipation and possibility in a ceramic cup.

These flawless dawn interludes are available every day of the year. In the hours before the details of the day begin, reading pages and using muscles is still the routine. These deliberate silent rituals and the pleasing specifics within each, such as sauntering along uneven trails or how the mornings play out, count for a lot. Yesterday, as I trekked the grass road up to the farm, up the wild and winding paths of the mountain, the bursting seasonal colours prompted another one of those smiles. There's a lot that summons exuberance within.

For one, accomplishment without racing against time produces a similar effect. Stopping for lunch and sprawling, dirty and tired, on the plateau overlooking the valley does too. Even resting my shoulders from the weighty lantana trimmer while absorbing the scenery and work ahead delivers. The work contributes to a meaningful life. It always did. But the changed steadiness of progress and flexible forward motion allow and inspire me to walk on. I'm replacing the rush with satisfaction in everything I do. At last, I can attend to things with focus and attention, undivided.

All along, my regard for quality and detail helped me. But during my burnt out and busy season, the details that others bypassed bothered me so much that I handled them anyway. I couldn't deliver three-quarters of a job; it had to far surpass "good enough". But here's the catch: to complete all tasks to the lofty heights I set in an overloaded state meant life had to give. I gave and gave, handing my freedoms away like coupons for the privilege of lying awake each night knowing I did my best. Seconds later, I'd be restless, ruminating about the next eighty-plus items waiting and proliferating.

The thing is, the details matter, but health, dreams and living are details too—the crucial ones. By accident, I missed the vital points for a bit there. That's alright. I'm here now. Momentum builds regardless of the errors under my belt; momentum and enjoyment build because of them.

Slower is my way forward. Even in the moments that seem like lulls, there's productivity unfolding. The momentary pauses are not pauses at all. They are the fleeting inhales where the important details live, transitions between experiences that I no longer need to hurry through to get to the next.

At this productive pace, anything's manageable, if not effortless. Either I'm right, reaching or high on exercise and the upbeats of life. My stint of muscling wheelbarrows up hills while accepting more calls and tasks and wondering what happened to my day or how I skinned my elbows and knees is in the past. The race is over. Advance in natural strides, at dawn and the whole day through. Exist in the details, relish them. On repeat I promise myself, *I'm done racing.*

6 September 2024

Awake

I'm awake and content before sunrise again, wrapped in the fleece blanket, reading by the old corner lamp. I woke earlier than usual, eager to embrace the day and my morning nook. Enthusiasm flourishes alongside the jasmine, replacing the old, under-watered confines of fatigue. This must be another welcome development in finding my feet. Go with it.

I'm rolling with the learning phase of my new role and loving it almost as much as being at home, confirmation that I chose well. What I envisioned as a transition has the potential to be lasting, a foundation, even permanent. I hope so, because my contentment's genuine. The harmonious compilation of work, play, fun, rest and creativity is a force I'm unable to quantify or measure.

In other news, I breezed through another month alcohol-free. At this rate, *elimination* will be my word of the year. I'll maintain my preference for moderation. What I let go in some areas I have gained in others. Less income and hours for more time; mid-level responsibility for reduced stress; professional opportunity for work outdoors; and busyness for calm where the essentials shine. Everything's a trade. What I was nervous about releasing in exchange for things of higher value felt risky until I went for it. I didn't expect happiness to catch me. The immediate rewards of self-preservation made changing the wrongs I once deemed acceptable a pleasant pursuit.

In the end, despite some areas of my life reducing, I have it all. Tolerating for the sake of familiarity limits the discovery of the encouraging pages of a way better book. The cover reads: *Choice isn't a Luxury*. It's a more giving genre, healing and this sweet storybook life. I'll read on.

7 September 2024

Rest is writing, writing is rest

As I write, Chase and Rusty compete to claim my lap. Chase's latest habit: nudging my notebook with his moist snout to create room for at least two paws, his chest and the weight of his full embrace. And he's up, resting across my legs and the page. He takes hanging close by seriously. A creek walk is likely this afternoon. They wait for the word, anticipation experts! Along the rocky creek bed they roam free, romping in and out of the forest, investigating anything that causes a rustle. Serious business. They patrol for movement as I walk behind, looking out for the kaleidoscope of butterflies that call the creek home. If I utter a mention of their favourite place, they know we'll head down soon.

Love and gratitude transfer from the chocolate brown kelpie draped over my lap. Chase's handsome brown and tan face rests below my neck, his eyes closed, and defining caramel brows relaxed. I'm stopping to hug the dog again. A quick hug isn't enough. He settles in, this guy. My notebook's on his glossy back. He doesn't mind; he's found his spot. Whatever works is fine by me too.

I don't plan what I'll write yet seldom run out of musings to unpack. Rest is writing and writing is rest. It's a luxury to write for as long as the day's commitments allow, to talk to myself without speaking a single word. Silence is the most angelic sound. Again, whatever works.

Despite many changes and relaxations, I'm still me. The heightened sensitivity that helped me achieve and wear myself out lives on. However, throughout this pilgrimage (sounds nicer than burnout), I'm uncovering how to master, not abuse, the strengths I possess. My awareness of and attention to detail, sensations and emotions isn't new. Although now, these immense feelings lead to different destinations within. All senses relay vivid and grand as the beauty in the details gracing my days internalises and expands. It may just be that time stops long enough for me to appreciate my surroundings when there's a twenty-eight-kilogram pup lounging across my lap! Dog or not, sensitivity works both ways, holding the potential to enhance or hinder.

My ability to examine, interpret and act on the detailed anatomy of a project with unwavering commitment to lifted outcomes can be a burden. A weakness, even. But it's also resilience, and far from a soft trait. It's an enhanced interpretation of what life hands me, with a caveat: the intensity drains.

Burnout resulted from prolonged overuse of the serving aspects and assets of my sensitivity. The assets that benefited me until they wore me thin. It's all well intended, akin to kindness that extends beyond what's deserved. I thrive on the challenge and immersion in each experience. My achievements revolve around gleaning detail and harnessing it to advance an outcome. Hence, becoming consumed by the wrong small stuff. I excelled for extended periods while burnt out. When I struggled as though I would soon falter, instinct told me to bear down. I had endless workloads to complete, but processing power, if used incorrectly, depletes.

This attention to everything except the pained state of my destructive ways left me lost in the load and needs of others. *Switched on* took on new meaning as my sensitivity both enlightened and injured me. For a while, I hopscotched between both extremes until I reclaimed control; until I applied my attention to living a full life. The lesson: ability isn't my justification to act or give. I may not have chanced upon this place if not for the byproducts of burnout and my sensitivities. The qualities that defined my outward success also broke me, and then saved me. I'm architecting an existence of broader dimensions, where my sensitivity gives more than it takes.

Today, sensitivity offers bonuses. My life comprises a collection of heartfelt essays, in which sensitivity finds the best words. I take off when I write, and attention's my innate knowing, leading me home. Nurture this special form of emotional smarts, the analysis of what's deep in your being. It will help you rest and glean meaning in the years ahead. I found more than I expected in surrender, when I allowed sensitivity to shine a brightness on a comforting internal abode. I'm here to stay. Chase thinks so too.

8 September 2024

Arrived

Hello, Sunday morning. Stretched out on my yoga mat, Rusty's lazing his way through the first hours of his day. He knows how to muster peace, and more often than not it involves some translation of what's mine becoming his. Weird dog aside, I expected my elation to fade. Instead, it flourishes, like the spring flowers following rain.

On arriving somewhere familiar yet foreign after a long, tiring but necessary trip, what I interpreted as inconsequential pit stops along the road turned out to be more. They were the sustenance and substance that delivered me here. It's my safe destination, having a life. The vibe is part first day of a holiday combined with receiving uplifting news. I was unaware I could choose circumstances to foster my joy and nothing more. I lacked the belief that living life this way was possible or even allowed.

Skipping towards abundance and away from threat, relaxing into myself means today belongs to me, tomorrow too. Next week is mine, as are the years to come. My task is to hold myself to the standards that maintain these freedoms, all that I changed and broke for, while they bud with returns.

This looks like being around for the kids long-term, waking and moving early, and a commitment to avoiding excess. It includes writing for pleasure and keeping nature as the backdrop in every frame. Deliberate action, learning, unlearning and questioning expectations and opinions, while treasuring the wealth I have. It's that too. But right now, it's chuckling as Rusty assumes an upward-dog pose with a smug wink and smirk as I move him over so we can share my mat. Sunday morning stretching and sunning under the canopy tree, the garden's largest green umbrella, is also his destination.

9 September 2024

Counting blessings and curating life

Two months on, and my to-do list looks different. It has new substance too—now it's more of a to-live list. With my priorities aligned, giving to what's important is the only default worth my time. The richness of my days correlates with the quality of my selections and curiosities. It's a scenario where everything flows.

I got the memo: a meaningful existence is attainable when there's opportunity to explore as well as do. I was a doer, so on task that I mistook tasks for fulfilment. Tasks and doing are not a life. At this stage, I'm a reformed doer—at least, a recovering one with a better list to substantiate it. The first page of my to-live list reads…

More

Handball games on the driveway.

Family dinners out.

Sunsets with a glass of wine on the back patio with Steven.

Trampoline jumps as high as we can bounce.

Little trips away within the new flexibility of our weeks.

Yoga under the sprawling trees.

Log fires, inside and out.

Running further, slower.

Board games and movie nights.

Candles lit, even during the week.

Sunrises in my dressing gown, alone.

Night walks to the horse park gate.

Fun.

Revisiting the books I adore the most.

Weekend chills together.

Adventures along the forest tracks shared by the families of kangaroos.

Time towards the farm project.

Reading, but limit your paperback order to one per fortnight if possible.

Broader art, music, points of view.

This all confirms that counting blessings and making conscious shifts in choice, perspective and environment curates a quieter life, one that nurtures. Choose with care, again and again. The faith I found and expanded in darkness played out as my final and vital task as a die-hard doer. The moments when no one was watching or needing became clusters of both grief and relief, galaxies of purpose, motivation and delight. I had to keep promises to myself, select well and be immune to giving my light away to meaningless obligation. About time.

Since topping up the twinkle in my world, an afterglow ensues. It mimics the exhilaration that follows exercise, but it lasts. Enacting my own rescue worked. Breaking for the wrong goals is where I failed. I failed when I didn't choose my family, when I permitted a job to take more than it should, when I became a task-driven doer lost in the dark. One day, I will express some version of all of this to others suffering for the unimportant—an addition for my list.

Noticing it all

I'm settling into my new routine—three days at work and four days of life, sometimes the other way around. It's not a far-fetched scene from a feel-good blockbuster. Nope, this is my life.

I'm structuring my free weekdays for writing and progress at the farm while the boys are at school. True to form, productivity is at the core of the narrative, this time on the side of a mountain. Weekends are real weekends, a concept so foreign I toy with the need for subtitles or an explanatory foreword for those sections of my story, but I'm resisting adding either. The gaps, the unstructured self-legislation and liberties—they're the plump, nutrient-dense fruits of change. Breathtaking things appear as if by accident when these pockets of downtime combine with the autonomy I'm structuring.

These mellow undulations of reality and emotion roll like soft surf swells, offering valuable observation of needs, cause and effect, of what to repeat, integrate and leave behind. They are the testing grounds for my transpiring plot, an exercise in noting and exploring what will stay. So far, so great encapsulates my mood, and questions about providential luck echo in my internal reel. From where I'm sitting, I'm holding aces. There are many reasons I feel this way, including school holidays, where I can make plans with the kids and also work. I no longer have to choose the wrong thing and talk myself into being okay with it. Turns out, I exacerbated major issues in the framework of my life's structure, script and score. Everything's better this way, and the brave edits add depth. Every day.

It's impossible not to notice my world overflowing with affirmative themes and tones. Two steps into tonight's early evening stroll, the dusk heavens turned blush lolly pink and baby blue. The hues behind the defined, fluffed clouds reflected through, creating fairy floss skies. I want more of this, to use my time and skills to hone life instead of handing it away. Aspirations for further refinement roll on too. Each action writes a part of the story so uplifting that the motivation to carry on is instinctual. I'm acclimatising, and this reality of genuine positivity is only the start.

11 September 2024

Ease doesn't equal easy

There's much I'm yet to grasp and ongoing opportunities for learning. I love this so much. I took a lot too seriously. I achieved, I delivered, obsessing and rechecking to be sure, like the chef who refuses to serve a plate without personality or memorable taste. It wasn't about perfecting each outcome, but about my effort being exemplary, every time. Despite making changes, this commitment to excellence works, so long as I vary the intensity.

I'm getting the hang of healing and recognising the tipping points in my life. To live well, to improve, calls for a continuous counterbalancing of self, an intricate interaction between pressure and pull. It's corny, but I get a lot out of counselling myself, and rest too is a worthy pursuit in recovering the hemispheres of everything I am.

Often, I picture myself sitting with a sagging soul at my desk, in my old sterile office, where I lived. I'm sorry for her. Not living, instead gripping the edges of slippery cliffs, in denial of the raging burnout falls around the bend. The waters miles ahead flow like an autumn weekend camping close to smooth stone banks. Although not in a tent, I'm proud of what I now refuse to accept, ignore and move past.

Do I line up with who I was—surface-level successful, there for many, but absent from those who needed me most? Yes, I'm enough across all segments of life as I integrate wellbeing with ease. No part of arriving here was linear, but to come full circle is to let doubt flee, defeated, back to my lived-in office seat. *Ease* wasn't easy to create, but called for, deserved and, above all, earned. Make it last.

14 September 2024

Heartwarming observations

Saturday trampoline jumps and chats with Leo and Rusty have already made my weekend, together with picking greenery from the garden to bring nature inside. The spanning leaves enrich a room. The grounds around home furnish supplies of foliage for every vase and pot I own. It's wealth by green measure.

Back to the day. The air's crisp as sunrays throw light on the moisture that adds to the aromas of trimmed grass. The dogs snooze, and I ponder. I now ponder!

The assortment of heartwarming observations inspires appreciation for this place I call home, sacred and sheltered by the trees. The nature-lined boundaries continue to burgeon in every conceivable tinge of earth and green. Despite the cycle of jasmine flowers, the wire borders remain lush and serene.

Havens like this allow access to creativity, recovery and life. There's no ignoring the grand trees with their decorative vines, winding and wrapping up the thick trunks, or the branches that fan to provide an ideal balance of sun and shade. Nature is art, with degrees of complexity and detail that humans can't forge. I won't leave this garden, the source of much healing. This spot will play a role in sealing and supporting an abundant future. Each breeze hints so. I didn't arrive here by accident. The discomfort and trip-ups eventuated to lift me, scooping me up and seating me here, pondering amongst the trees.

My physical pain had a purpose, as a protective mechanism and motivator of action to defend and promote recovery. The psychological aches throbbed and compelled change in the same way. However, these aches were subjective, hidden, not localised to a visible spot. A hurt mimicking a strong pulse, these vibrational sadnesses, the currents of emotional fragility deep within. It's why I fell; pain forced me to stop for my own good.

In front of me is a generous natural world, with a lot of lawn. Similar to the reassuring and gentle movements throughout the garden, time also progresses, flowing, and free. This is what faith feels like. There's no concrete evidence, but divine new meaning around courage, trust, connections and comfort zones.

17 September 2024

The journey away from suffering

A Tuesday morning sleep-in because we can. School holidays together at the beach, enjoying the sun and over-salted beach kiosk fish and chips from the paper, sandy and sun-kissed before heading home. Oh, and prolonged cuddles every day.

Dedication and consistency deserve these priceless rewards, though consistency itself is often the ultimate bounty. The correct priorities make life whole. Health and wellness, not counting the odd piece of battered fish, are about time with my family. Once too stressed and employed to take part, I let the ordinary yet extraordinary pass me by, my devotion to my work disproportionate. I dismissed that for longer than healthy.

Skip forward a few valuable and transformative months to here, where intuition guides my decisions and peace is the prize. I'm not torn or at anyone's disposal without question or considered thought. Although my answer is yes to a lot, unavailable is my status of choice. Sounds harsh, but it serves us as a family. My mindset and self-talk are shifting too, with soft reminders steadying me here and there. I'm careful to take action and walk on between the reading and absorbing. Forward motion settles doubts, aiding in the release of who I was.

More good is on the horizon, like the invigorating smell ahead of heavy, sustaining rain. Opportunities change as I change. I'm thankful for that. It shows there are no restrictions or restraints on lofty goals or elemental truths. Things will come as they should, nothing forced, nothing missed, only security that I've got this. I'm living my best life far from bewildering overwhelm. Vitality's increasing. Short of landing splat in an exhausted heap, I may have accepted "familiar, unhappy, but oh-so needed" as normal for the rest of my life.

Hence, burnout's a confronting yet imperative offering, providing both an exit and an entry. If I were religious, my words would spell *thank God*. There's a chance I'm more open to that than I thought. It's difficult not to be when the Universe carries on recreating everything in my favour.

To hold proof that letting go, no matter the investment made, strengthens and enlightens, is as beautiful as our morning together playing on the sand. There's no sunk cost, only growth in the experience.

18 September 2024

Trying before knowing

If only I'd known all I know now, before. What a difference that might have made! But that's not how life goes. Trusting and trying prior to knowing, while difficult, was the best way. There are likely vast cities and suburbs of broken people unsure what to do to help themselves, asking if change holds potential to deliver a kinder fate. I assume there are many like me. I wasn't aware my life could transform. Do they have any idea? I hope so, because the gloomy chambers of burnout were a low and lonely place, a cold basement car park on a wintry night. Internalised wounds, avoidance, denial, doubt and blind acceptance all park there.

From what I could tell, there's no community warning systems at those depths, when surrounded by cold concrete underground.

Only my own alerts telling me to exit, relaying as a scrambling static at first. It got louder and easier to decipher, but I was too empty to escape up the stairs towards change and air. Even when I wanted to take power back, change felt daunting and unfamiliar, so I conserved energy and remained in my garage of guaranteed overwhelm for longer.

I almost didn't save myself. I almost didn't try or reach. Seeing a prelude of what change brings would've helped. I owe thanks for the eye-openers that came in time, some so inspiring and symbolic of how far I've come that I revisit them, ensuring I move forward and not back.

First up, I now know that any form of intense prolonged stress is a warning not to ignore. Sometimes I need to make deletions and removals. My status quo had little chance of improving. Difficult to face, but healing fell to me, tired or otherwise. In acting, my resolve took care of the stamina required from there. It didn't seem so, but I had a lot left within. Resilience endured.

In no way did I imagine that the deepest discomforts were signposts, pointing away from the path I was on, there to compel change and retreat. From my once clueless point of view, irritation communicated that I should give more, but I had other options, many I walked past and over, unaware. Actual four-leaf clovers were abundant throughout the ground cover when I took the time to look.

Never again will I underestimate my ability to question or choose. Had I acted earlier, I would've seen I had no reason to fear. Save yourself early in the future; don't work to fix circumstances that feel wrong. The weight lifted the moment I shut that door on that Friday night in July. Memorialise that feeling, your example of change working out. When *poised* transitions to *withdrawn*, listen and move. My inability to keep hiding pain isn't an invitation to press on. Instead, to adjust. A dense haze of stress isn't normal or acceptable. Few can thrive in continuous fog, and another, another, another stressful season is a pattern to inspect. Turns out I wasn't defective, and beneath the veil of anxiety existed the real me.

Last of all, this next awareness debunks my theories about pleasing others (and myself). I didn't expect everyone around me to validate my decision to walk away, but they did. Validation and support were available *because* I stopped people-pleasing. Who would have thought? The personal work is my most valuable project of all, and new doors keep opening—smaller, exciting ones. Ambition also returned, although it went nowhere. It grew, and I didn't feel lost for long. I felt sure.

The experience became enjoyable, and life today is more than okay. Imagine understanding all of this sooner, amid breakdown. A return to burnout is unlikely; surviving it is my dose of efficacy and prevention in one shot. Somehow, burnout and its trimmings make sense, and meaning exists in everything I encountered and braved. I feared change until change revealed my world, like a spectacular flower maturing in slow motion.

How gratifying to admit I have no regrets in trusting myself, despite uncertainty about where each choice may lead. How fortunate that each deep breath infuses more delight, tasting of fresh-picked mint in crisp soda over ice. And for those still stuck, finding their own version of these truths could be the difference between trying and trusting change or not. Ready or not. Sure or not. It could be the distinction between healing or not.

20 September 2024

Finding balance in the wobbles

By the fire pit on this Friday night, arranging my thoughts on the page. The oversized cast-iron bowl radiates warmth, matching the terracotta glow of the flickering flames. Immersion in a charming image from my Pinterest board would be like this. Except this is real. I'm there.

With our chairs close, Steven and I chat and stay warm. He exudes his chilled vibe that relaxes me too (most of the time). There's something on my mind that I need his perspective on.

"Hey, it's a worry the blocks of land are taking longer to sell than planned," I venture.

"Yep," he says. "We got it done, held them through Covid and beyond, and now that we want to move them on, it's a muck around.

Don't worry; they'll sell. The next offers won't be duds, and we have savings. It will be fine, but the entire project still feels like a failure."

"I know."

Profound shared disappointment aside, it helps to know we're almost there. So close, thanks to our extended efforts and the many big pushes that came before. Despite the complications and compromises, the upcoming financial security that selling the land will provide is an incredible outcome and option to have. *Don't worry so much*, I remind myself.

The realisation, spoken in silence between our eyes and touching palms, is that every experience leads somewhere, adding value in roundabout yet meaningful ways.

Knowing this, as I sit here reflecting on the giving ruins of my previous existence, I'm accepting. It's part of history in my private museum. This exhibition, which depicts the realities of life, drew diverse subjects from those experiences. If I'd done things differently, I wouldn't be arriving here. My contrasting emotions—between past struggles and tonight's contentment—mark the journey. They mark growth.

Now and again, the two early pregnancies we lost before Jackson became our world flash back. In the grief and loss, we navigated all that accompanies heartbreak. The news of no heartbeat stopped mine for a moment as the cold ultrasound gel enhanced my shivers of anguish. In that piece of my past, nature had its reasons for a temporary pause, although it cut closer to cruel spiritual abandonment. But those experiences aligned with our beautiful boy, the baby meant for us. The lessons and missteps add substance, if they were even missteps at all. Either way, they contribute to my chronicle of both demanding and encouraging humanity.

It's easy to compartmentalise and reflect from a nicer place, fireside with the moon in full view above the dense backlit treetops. But that's the whole point—to appreciate how far I've come, to be warmed. Appreciation followed hardship. The lows cultivated and emphasised it. Not at the time, but in time, as each challenge became history. I'm balancing out, experiencing enough to respect that value lives at either end of the extremes.

The richness of my life relies on the wobbles. The teetering up, down, back, forward and sideways creates the balanced average or mean. To experience each state and return to a stabilised emotional norm is part of balance as well. Wholeness and balance don't revolve around rest and comfort alone. Without the tough tales, my highs mean less. Worth and appreciation diminish, and if that happens, my balance tips towards bland.

The ranges I traversed were essential. To make it here, I had to grow as I broke. I had to encounter enough to learn what to leave behind in the galleries of past times. This night, at some point, will also become history, catalogued in my museum. That future exhibit will pay homage to these adventures, love and moonlight included. The object on display will be a delicately complex pencil sketch of a full and healthy heart relaying a journey through catharsis and self-love.

22 September 2024

I notice more

This stage—the middle of my life, the body of my full story—it's unique. My developing personality strengthens as it grows. This is my time of reduction and simplification, my chance for refuelling and recalibration. Midlife—that is, post clearing the mess I produced (and perfected). My days feature a fresh and growing abundance. Thank you! Is it a natural part of midlife or because I'm paying attention?

In my current state, I'm like a sapling mature enough to be tagged robust. I'm done with chaos, and the free-for-all towards boundless external service is over, too. The goodness collects and assures there is brightness and thriving self-loyalty ahead.

Operating this way holds power. Perfection is not my end goal because nothing's flawless, but everything is right. I am grounded in my renewed ability to focus, even during the little stresses too, the sort that pass with the task. As they should. This is an unfamiliar experience, where attention and effort return validating signs and calls. Confirmations arrive all day long. I'm mending everything, insecurities included. The past isn't bad; rather, it's a challenging patch of distanced choppy whitecaps that comprise my life.

How I live today is serene in comparison. It's a place where beauty and freedom come alive in silence and space. It's in the hush of the mornings and afternoons, when the crickets and the breath of the slight breeze vibrate, dominating with ease. I get to experience this awe, no longer consumed and needed with no end or boundaries known. The ability to ignore is a skill. Paying attention is as well. At least I know I have what it takes to make improvements through change.

Insights galore today, as I counterbalance the dog on my lap. Again. The whole-dog approach obliges an unhurried afternoon. We'll stay here on the patio, where the moss acts as mortar between the clay pavers, for a while longer gazing down the yard. Thanks for the tender reminder, Rusty Dog, for another reason to watch the world go by.

Normal is not always nice

If slower serves, what have I pushed myself for? For all these years. More belongings, funds, responsibility, more stress. I traded life for things, the pride of a title included, unaware that what is normal is not always nice.

Did I strive for the sake of it? To strive to strive is an exhausting and jilted maze with few roads out. But there was another way. I reserved rest for special occasions that may not come. With *busy* and *in demand* etched in bold on my creed of success, I bought it, the alluring lie of upper management. Work a ton, accelerate, accumulate. I excelled at that too, working up to a pace that destroyed me.

Less is lazy. I toyed with this notion more than once. To do more is progress. To do less is, well, less. I performed to my potential, applying *perform* in the literal sense, feeding a lifestyle that admires burnout. My potential—reaching the limits of breakdown and collapse. I got that far. I didn't understand how skewed that rendition of normal was until I exited that panicked life. Normalising overwork was worse than allowing others to expect it from me. I don't even think they did expect it. I buried myself, which is by far the saddest part of my story. To my surprise, burnout, the outcome of my irresponsibility, grabbed me by the shoulders in time.

Big thanks to the Universe (again) because what I celebrate today differs a great deal. This week I worked three days and covered essential expenses. A fair trade. I returned income relative to the time invested, didn't spend on materialistic excess, and savoured experiences with the kids. I had opportunities for exercise and progress, and I didn't rush; I enjoyed the days. Be it sitting in the sun or working in the garden, I lived.

It took me a while, but I'm discovering the price of calm—somewhere close to half my previous wage. The portion that I saved. I have responsibility with healthy and respected limits, ones I don't need to enforce; they exist on their own. Once again, there's an aura of fun attached to productivity. Perhaps this is what normalcy is, and my situation was atypical.

I have trouble pinpointing why I didn't move in this direction sooner, where showing kindness to myself is a priority. Money matters. Choices matter. It all matters. There are certain realities, such as required income and everyday responsibilities that I can't avoid and I don't want to. I adore work and even miss the intellectual aspects of my old role, but not at the expense of all else. Occasionally, I miss working at the top of my game in an industry I know inside out and achieving beyond my own expectations, but to say I've done it is enough, and cultivating such clarity, a relief.

Change is a permanent win. I did that. Nothing is out of reach. I'm strong because I'm sure. The one thing more dopamine-inducing than confirming I made the right moves is knowing I can make more. This is a far more pleasing normal, one where I'm free and accomplished while achieving wider versions of success. My belief system's undergone revisions, reading more like a melody than a mandate, a softer trail in place of a detrimental trajectory to perceived prosperity.

Odd but true: the best feedback, the valuable praise from self and others, came from trusting another way. Continue removing and continue to gain. Keep replacing obligation with space. Trade-offs exist, but they are worth whatever I gave up. What if I gave up nothing at all, but gained back what I'd given up all along? Consider that.

30 September 2024

Hope as a Tool

Love in motion is farewelling Jackson off on his first school camp today. It's inhaling the pure scent of his just-washed hair as he presses in for two days' worth of kisses in the bustling school hall.

Side thoughts as we embrace: I found a magnificent inner sanctum where everything makes sense. Self-determined interventions—they're monumental, and I won't go back. The plethora of big questions, the ones I now contemplate, holds power. Control and comprehension are back with me. I can be anyone I choose, with no prospect of choice eroding.

It's fair to say pain relayed stranger than imagined: jarring, uncomfortable, off. I kept pressing the black sharp and flat keys on life's piano, over the ivory natural notes. Each fallen tear spoke its own truth while streaking down my face. As I heed the messages and sounds, progress transpires in my in-tune sovereign state. I'm unstuck, which trumps trashing more years clinging to what's ceased to serve me. In trading money for minutes and moments, I'm taking my future back. With this comes more hope, amplified.

Warm experiences combined, life's a gathering of gives and takes with euphoric moods and lifted states. I'm emerging from some emotional chrysalis, harnessing my new so-called wings, if that's even a thing. I know who I am and approve of who I'm becoming as I put my hope-endowed tools to use.

My subconscious attracts what I seek—these rewards of presence are delivered daily. "Love you, J," I tell my little boy. "Have the best time."

"Love you too, Mum. I'll miss you guys, but I'll have fun," he says, wiping his few tears on my cream T-shirt, and that's that.

3 October 2024

My world continues to lift

My thoughts drift to how I can offer something to others now that I'm done resuscitating myself. I have more to give. My aim is that my experience lends someone a hand or even a telescope to marvel at the remarkable emotional nurseries that can follow pain. My lived example illustrating an enchanted way through burnout if one pays attention to the signs might help.

However, with my piles of full journals, will I have the courage to share? This question brings about more. Is the quality there? Would anyone gain from reading this? Could anyone bear to read it? Is there a book amongst the scribblings of an unknown nobody who is as insignificant as a ladybug going about her day on a random leaf in spring? It's a pretty juicy leaf, succulent in sustenance and form. Please may my story give like that one day.

For now, it's of little concern. The fact I'm uncertainty's biggest fan, even more than I was of Hanson in my teens, is the only answer I need. I write to navigate, process and progress. The outcome will work itself out, and it could also be the precise point—that healing lives in my actions and rituals, not the net results or accolades. My pain was private; that's how it hurt me the most. But my repair worked well behind closed doors, within, alone, offering reverent reclaim. Whatever happens later, documenting my way is proof of my refreshed life. I like that, and although the safe choice is to hold back, one day I'd like to say I'm a writer by burnout's default.

8 October 2024

Escapism no longer required

reetings to this moody and bordering-on-humid afternoon as a storm prepares to roll in. The sky's electric aura signals there's an event coming soon, as if the power lines feeding the house also energise the clouds. Nature leans into the upcoming weather with full acceptance. It's quite an approach.

The atmosphere, the air, radiates fresh but thick as the dense raindrops hit the roof and caress the trees. Inside, I'm safe and sheltered, in all interpretations of the phrase. The ambiance of home reassures, as soothing as the incoming showers. The halo of ease wrapping everything is visible if I pay close attention. This newfound abundance of light extends far and wide, with bounds I don't want to breach. Beauty amplifies here. Rushing is absent from each morning's roll call, and I'm stronger as the days pass. This way of life, it's as evocative as the supreme sights combined. Everything's well and alive.

For one, the curvature of the stem holding the torso-sized leaf plucked from the garden lets it peep around the corner, out of the vase and towards the yard. It, too, wants to sway in the dolloping rain. Or the perfume from the triple-wick gardenia candle wafting to enhance each corner of the room. Or the reassurances ever-present in the pages touched and turned. Even the comfort food roasting and the kids coming and going at their will from one outdoor activity to the next with little care for the rain exude a palpable energy.

I finally see it—the definite connection between the physical world and what it conjures within. If I let it. To say it best, to best relay the condition, *blessed* is the word.

Before, I missed so much. So much good. I felt well regarded, but not powerful. Not the power that translates to status or the final say, but strength within, belief that I'm in charge of my life. Self-esteem, a sureness in abilities, yes, but I conditioned myself unable to choose life over a list.

In protecting no limits, I disappointed myself for decades over letting anyone down. I gave away personal power, obligation by obligation, knowing I could do what's needed whenever others asked. Of course, if *I* asked, needed, sought, I didn't jump to attention until I had no choice. At some point, givers require solace too.

Then came burnout, the catalyst that introduced me to the power I held but squandered with grace, forcing me to develop a tenacity for self, not for a job. To turn my skills within, to walk with more than my tippy toes touching the ground, to stare in the mirror long enough to see.

Sad, the deflated reflection reminded me of a long-journeyed and parched bird. It made me question my reality, direction and all. Change or break, heal or spiral, migrate to a kinder climate or risk it all. Navigating those misty skies appears dangerous upon review. I avoided the wrong turns thanks to the helping tailwinds guiding me along.

There's a lot I'm unable to explain, but whatever I did, it's working. I'm recuperating from my punishing long-haul, not flapping to escape my circumstances. Instead, I'm leaning in, taking inspiration from nature (and my past mistakes) ahead of afternoon spring storms. The cue is to keep going, to welcome the subtle lessons from the pieces and pages of recovery, from these episodes of reclaiming the freedoms and basics of life.

9 October 2024

If nature could talk

I f nature could talk, it would say, *Stay here, right here, learn from me. Use my offerings to bolster stamina and awe via observation. Use them to fortify the vertebrae that form the* backbone of genuine joy.

Stop to nose the native bush flowers and consume the thriving herbs amongst the huddles of garden pots.

Add generous sprigs of homegrown rosemary to chunky-cut potatoes and to botanical gin, sometimes.

Marvel at the reaching branches of hardy trees and let the earth move in between the valleys of your toes.

Listen to the rain, breathe it in, inhale and let it refresh and remind you of clean slates, renewal, and the washing away of *obsolete things. This is necessary. Seek grass that's sure to brush your leg or cushion your head as you lie back and gaze at the canopies that decorate the sky.*

Watch me transform as you transform, with compassion and regard for the infinite connected parts. As the leaves fall with the wind, flow too with each gentle movement of change. You'll land where intended, in some part of the cycle of life.

Nature knows, so venture amongst the many groves and river-banks that my tracks and your maps will help you find. Nothing's without reason. Each element has its place, its linkage to the outcomes. There's room for rebirth and fluctuations, the ones that have to occur before each nightfall, season and dawn.

What endures and persists does so for significance to the larger whole. The hidden root and nutrient systems tell wondrous stories and offer hints aboveground.

Cycles matter, as do the collectives of microscopic changes that carry impact enough to prompt regeneration and growth. The nonessential sheds and becomes something else to sustain what must survive or sprout again. There's space for differences and competing needs.

These natural frictions compel solutions, compromise and fertile diversity throughout the lands.

Protection from the elements follows the ability to withstand bleak and difficult times, and warmth replaces the preceding seasons of cold. Prepare to hold on. In time, everything passes, and things either regenerate or cease. Life comes back to life, often in a new form. Look, listen and watch with intent as there's sustenance and meaning in the tiny specks the human eye gets to see.

Nature tells me to trust it as the source and to let everything be. It reminds me to give ear to my intuition, alive and well within, because it too will continue to deliver.

My reply to nature is that I'll remain a grateful student in the outdoor study halls of life. My notebook is open and ready as I listen to your words.

10 October 2024

Perspective is the difference

While cultivating burnout, I thought if I did everything right, everything would be alright, until it wasn't. I worked mighty hard to bolt down a perfect-looking mainstream path, the one destined for me, where the manicured hedges alongside conformed like perfectionists in a row. Those neat hedges hid a lot.

On my way, I achieved with utmost diligence, careful to colour within the lines. I had options to exit, to choose a quieter life, but I didn't. Instead, I broke. Repetitive questions haunted me every night. *How did I get here? Where is the exit? What will those who rely on me think?*

I encouraged myself to find a way. A way to do more. With no hours left, and the weeks more than spoken for, the situation compounded, outdoing itself as compounding does. Reminders that my family needed me came in flashes. They noticed my distress, but I turned straight back to work, certain I had no choice but to continue. Then, I broke some more. Too busy to function was yet another perplexing enigma of my stress.

Burnout didn't announce itself or let me know as it arrived. That recognition landed later, although I knew something wasn't right. I weighed how to come to terms with throwing my career away. For a break? Ridiculous, that's not me. I push on, not over. Then, I broke some more.

Navigating major life decisions in a state of impending collapse was like limping to safety with multiple hairline fractures following months of no sleep. Confronting. I wanted it to stop but didn't know how to withdraw. The wildflower and butterfly-laden path that's obvious now wasn't always so. I entertained poor solutions and wasted time scrutinising how I'd explain burnout if I had to.

Preserving the wisps of me that were left needed to happen earlier. Relief followed my near-lifeless step over to this alternative way I'm naming *Save Yourself Lane*. Perspective and hindsight are miraculous things. I've found my place and a healthier point of view.

11 October 2024

Impressive imperfection

Thoughts while driving today…

Conversations about motherhood, life and choices confirm that we are all alike. Somewhat lost, wearing many hats and imperfect, we are human. I chose and created the conditions I thought I wanted. Busy was routine, and rest secondary to the obligations of frantic, overstimulated days. Reason and purpose existed amid every challenge and effort. That's what I told myself anyway. But what reverberates the loudest is the conflict and confusion between what to prioritise and where to give next because it all takes precedence; everything's important. I worshipped that falsehood too.

As the boys grew and manageability returned, I donned a few more hats. And so, my rotation around ten different suns continued. Any time that I gained back was diluted and distributed, evaporating into vapour. While building a life, I missed much life. To deliver more for the privilege of additional work isn't success; it defines getting played.

In striving for it all, I worked beyond limits, tended to a home I had fleeting opportunities to enjoy and hustled together meals I rarely savoured. I wasn't there, or anywhere. Presence was the dream; the fantasy was that I'd do better next week, so I kept going, questioning whether it was best to cry, laugh or lie flat on my back for a minute or two.

In an age where burnout's as common as a Netflix subscription, shared human imperfections are the undercurrent of my story. Among other things, burnout's shown me to adjust when needed. Doing less is not weak. It's smart. Not selfish, but wise and well thought out, strategic even. It's seizing the irreplaceable stages with the kids and protecting time with them, and myself.

Instead, I took on extra days, managed larger teams and did more until all-round fatigue left me scratching my head asking *far out, what for?* Silly and so unnecessary. Thankfully, relatability helps, as in, no one copes all the time. Impressive enough is staying upright or standing back up if I fall. This is me rallying, imperfectly!

12 October 2024

The schedule is by… me

It took courage to admit I was having a difficult time. That admission was about six months ago. Today, I exist differently.

When I was work-walking through my precious life, months passed in a flash. I was unconscious. Admission felt like failure at first, a crushing form of defeat. Burnout got me; no denying that. Funny, though—as I failed in one sense, I won.

The way existed in the truth sessions with myself and select others, in accepting help. To move on, to mend the broken parts of me, took a lot, but change, the last resort left to embrace, is how I found my place.

Burnout doesn't detract from my past. Arrangements of wins defined those years, and I can't discount that. Difficulties and peaks pass, and now and again they linger and last. I'd made it, yet I had no peace. Meeting peace was a discovery of the tenderest kind, similar to realising you've never been in love as you come face to face with the love of your life.

During my courtship with peace, I'm recording hundreds of thousands of pen strokes on healing and how I got so lucky. The words are like my unicorn, the white one in my thoughts way back when, delivering me to where I'll stay. I didn't consider finding my way through the haze feeling as though I'm on the back of some snowy, otherworldly version of a horse.

Life's surprising, especially now. I'm a different person thanks to experience and change, my high-functioning stress tamed. Step one was reaching for the reins and waving for a little help. Normalised tolerances take time to release, and more ease enters as I relax my grip. My sources of light at this time include…

Bedtime snuggles with the boys while giggling at our answers to funny questions. Leo's innocence when asked to declare something fun about himself stays front of mind. "Mum, I'm the best at staring competitions, but sometimes I have long staring comps with my soft toys and they never lose."

The rust colour of the tree trunks when the first drops of rainstorms make contact.

Home, alone or together.

Discovering an epic author who has a series of books.

The folded bottom pages of chapters to revisit.

A heavy blanket when the day's done.

Carbs.

The euphoria that follows a productive early morning.

Day in, day out confirmation that choice is my prerogative.

The smile on my face despite new grey hairs and developing wrinkles.

Choosing challenges and focusing, free from constant interruption.

The waft of espresso as it hits my cup and sipping it alone before anyone's up.

The compounding cues that corroborate I'm doing well.

A full stop at the end of the sentence *no thanks*.

Paying attention to *my* life and knowing I have options.

This list isn't conclusive, but it marks this stage well enough. I can revisit as I please because the schedule is by... me.

13 October 2024

Elevations of awareness

Contemplation brings clarity, although not everything needs to be rationalised. Sometimes there's no answer, no conclusion to draw, and it's okay for there to be things I don't understand. I won't try to answer some questions I have about certain situations. Scenarios lacking sense do so because they weren't where fate intended me to stay. Every so often, stuff just happens, and total resolution needn't be the goal. Overthinking, squandering energy decoding every circumstance, serves no purpose. It steals from the moment, from the fairy tale I now call home. It all mattered—chaotic yet structured, instrumental but punishing, each stage unfolded the way life planned. Hold close the knowledge that it helps me grow.

Despite growth, the achiever within hints I could've done more. For myself, for others, for my future. Then I recall the trophies of a steady, sustainable life. This *is* me doing more, more of what enriches the portrayal of the dearest form of art. The art of living well.

I'm eager to achieve more. What those things are is shifting, but anything of value demands the commitment I've long given. Some days play out that way; I accomplish much, and others fall short, but now with valid cause. How good! I'm free to choose, not helpless against an agenda that made a habit of sweeping me off my feet, and not in a romantic sense. If something bumps to tomorrow, it's because something more important needed to take its place today. The overload of the irrelevant doesn't stifle what should chief the rest.

Time for money sounds simple, and it should be. The lines blur when the timer doesn't stop, when you stay *on* after each triathlon-like day. My position paid me well to cover distances and tackle expanses of difficult ground, but not for nonstop legs scheduled for completion each day at noon because the next race begins at 12.01 p.m. When there's no one to cover you, but you cover everyone else, you're it, dejected with no leeway for a breath. At my new cadence, interactions no longer result in colossal workloads heaped on. Everything is minimalistic, arranged with intention. Imitation happiness never once felt this genuine. My happily ever after transpires as I heal.

Early hours of 14 October 2024

White blank pages of joy

The freedom each page allows determines the substance of life. On paper, anything's possible. Exploration, options, responses to uncertainty, and the rest. The act brings resolution and value, not what's written. Some days the pages read bland and repetitive, other days, I'm proud of what I explore and actualise.

Now and again, freedom comes with doubt about whether working less long-term is a cop-out. What about the money I could earn? The financial implications are manageable, but real. It's a process of ongoing and considered choice, but overall, I remain elevated. Regardless of life's minor tensions, I'm buoyant when I write.

I haven't told many people how writing pulled me from burnout's pit. There's fear in admitting I recorded it all. It's raw and regards intimidating aspects of the human condition, exploring my flaws in vulnerable detail, but there's a shared humility in that. The words scribed went from sad and strained to one day beautiful. The journey was much the same. Unexpected yet splendid, like my favoured role as life's scrivener.

As the misery dissolved, new possibilities ushered me back to self. To arrive through words, to craft feelings and experiences together on paper, soothes. It opens the doors to a greater purpose, which seldom exists without the happenings that came prior. There's reason in it all.

Indeed, what might be my calling, beyond revelling in writing, which ignites everything in me? Is it to communicate that fulfilled lives exist if we're brave or fed up enough to curate them? What worked for me was change because of pain. I maxed out the capacity to know who I was, what I liked. Lost in some bizarre emotional place, fading and unsure. The epiphany I received was: do the opposite of what you know. So, I stopped, listened and changed. I dove into the uncertainty, trusting I'd emerge well. I did the opposite of what I'd usually do.

Through writing and reading, I processed and faced the decisions I had to make. Low in trust of my ability to think, I surrendered and let the words bring me back. Return to clarity is a breathtaking experience, back to lands long ago roamed. For months, that resembled jotting pages and pages of unsettling and flowing thought. Breakthroughs surfaced one entry at a time.

Each day built on the last as I shut parts of myself down to unlock others. Discovering that choice is mine made burnout worthwhile, despite hard. For more than a while, I sought resilience to endure, but I needed the gumption to ride away into the twilight, to move on. Realisations became turning points, and each turning point encouraged change, directions guiding me home.

Diverse approaches exist in every situation. Retreating inward when something's not working isn't selfish. It's a requirement. No one was coming to fix how I operated. Only I had that power, and I used it. If I hadn't, conflict pledged to continue. Hindsight imparts that breakdown wasn't all terrible. Rather, it was a chance, an invitation suggesting that a stroll along the quieter path is both wise and advised. I can deliver like before if I want to, but these days I also work for myself.

My job is less, and I like it. There's latitude in my days. Ambitious, sure, but I collect confirmations each time I decline options to return to a larger role. As I fill the pages, I replenish. Each white leaf and notebook of sheets asks me to bring to life the warming tutorials of self-belief. Writing is tactile thinking therapy that underlines the joys of simplicity. It's confirmation that less can render me hand-on-heart grateful for being grateful. The mounting pages showcase all I'm thankful for. My journals are my thank you note to the Universe, my unsophisticated version of prayer, my way of expressing gratitude for being aware. I'm a participant in my life. I'm in a safe place. The statuesque ginger plants scattered throughout the garden emit the same flowering welfare, adorning the yard with their ornamental clusters, everywhere.

Mid-morning, 14 October 2024

All on me

I got myself into a mess, but I also boosted myself out. I moved here. That responsibility's equal parts physical, spiritual and emotional. It took work, tears, discomfort and the patience of a saint. Patience doesn't top my list of skills and attributes, but there's a chance I misinterpreted that.

To trade my situation, the platinum season-ticket level of burnout, for an upgraded life required time infused with loyal dedication to self-education. This outlay, it repays. I navigated and mended with my confidants—movement, books, nature, writing and rest. On repeat and repeated some more. No hacks or half-baked attempts. I invested all to pivot from nowhere to here.

At first, my short-circuiting fight-or-flight nerves, the shock of change and the curtain closing on the life I knew kept me moving and awake. I refused to fall in a heap for longer than a few days. My advice to self: start as I intend to continue. Self-care ranked as crucial, but not at the expense of action. Many of those essential initial moves registered as miniature steps in a new direction. With to-do checklists no more my world order, I created other registers (in my head). Rebuild list, curiosity catalogue, limits index, like-to-do directory. I exchanged needy inboxes for acute wellness accountability across my roles as a mother, wife and daughter.

In retrospect, those first weeks of total checkout became as vital as air. I prioritised what I needed and closed down anything with the potential to hinder my progress. Apart from removing myself from my job, the other major changes included where I gave my energy, how much I volunteered for, and what I was willing to self-impose.

The requirement I guarded as astutely as a bird protects her young was that each action had to serve recovery. I removed everything that didn't and substituted with what did. Calm growth prevailed as the selection criteria. My plan had nothing to do with numbing or ignoring the origins and aftermath of burnout. I embraced the chance to examine my life, with the expectation of improving.

Healing's been an experience of opposites. I unearth meaning while abandoning what once meant so much. I reap as I release, retract yet expand, and I live more as I plan and orchestrate less. And it sounds backwards, but I'm discovering my worth as I reduce income.

The most apparent contradiction: I had to fall apart to come together. The exhaustion that complements burnout closed my mind. It left no room. Beyond tired, I made the room and kept going, for me. Initially, that's all it took. What once worked no longer does, and won't again because my vision, mission and purpose don't link to a vocation. They align with the person I'm becoming. And so far, learning how to twirl personal disarray into a state of wonder is part of the reverence.

Another great day

More spring storms added to the day, followed by another impressive rainbow to round it out. These are the best days. Even nature emits an invigorating vibe. Marvel at that.

From wearing myself thin to steeping peppermint tea while dinner cooks at dusk—I'm transferring my amazement at what's transpired onto the page. The writing itself pays respect to the unlimited potential for more days like these. Today I visited the library to be around books, because I can. I also walked the forest track and shared lunch with Steven before picking up the kids. Bless this culmination of things those with a life get to do. During lunch, we spoke without interruption, not in passing, but face to face, eye to eye. Revolutionary. Impromptu relationship-nourishing sessions for two occur more often—yet another beneficial outcome of change.

The reason is that I'm here, present in the conversations I'm having. I no longer miss the indistinct subtleties that encompass love and companionship or the multifaceted brilliance of the man who's long been in my corner. I love him as much as ever, but I now have opportunities to experience what that means. Our connection suffered when I sprinted the round-the-clock runways of the work world.

The benefits don't stop there. There's much about living this way that's delightful, like cooking a barbecue dinner outside with the boys as the sun sets on a random weekday afternoon. A vast change from having my afternoons accounted for months in advance. Add to this our extended chats, card games and laughs. Plus, collecting my babies from school and talking on the way home instead of missing it all or having to take another call the second they're in the car, ahead of more work as we unlock the front door. The distinction between lives settles me.

From this new place, I attempt many times over to rationalise my reasons behind my stressful past life, but I can't anymore. The further I move away, the tougher it is to defend and explain my choice to break myself in the name of achievement and praise. I assume that's the breakthrough, my inability to justify giving everything to a cause that wasn't mine.

Post breakdowns and breakthroughs, I have time for everything; nothing's overdone. The recurring verdict is: I want to write to provide for my brain and enhance the likelihood of more great days, of vibrant skies tomorrow and beyond. I'll make sense of the rest as I go, when the season's right. I'm open to welcoming new things but also appreciating what's taking shape—a new self-portrait in written form.

16 October 2024

Was change even that scary?

Sorting through old photos from 2021 to now reminds me that without change, I might have wound up far beyond broken, with little to show for it. With change, I had a chance. I smiled like I was happy enough, but I wasn't. The disguised suffering in my eyes in the otherwise joyous pictures isn't invisible to me anymore.

At the outset, my thoughts of change mimicked a hurricane of what-ifs, philosophical questions and worst-case scenarios circulating rampageous and fast. However, from where I stand today, change wasn't that scary. Much of what I assumed was a big deal doesn't make my radar anymore. Opinions mean less, and intuition stays on as a sincere guide. I'm not worried about what worrying is doing to me, further proceeds of transformation obvious in more recent photos.

Most of the rewarding parts of my past were hard, and now and again resistance still joins my sundry crew of doubt and scepticism, too. But if I could usher myself through change knowing what I do now, I'd have much to share given the challenges I've faced and adjustments I've made.

To start, I would assure the woman in those pictures that moving towards another option if things aren't sitting right is okay. Finding a nicer avenue through is possible. Do it. Similar to meditation attempt number 139, it will make sense in time.

Also, pay attention to any in-your-face, strange gut feelings, oversteps and telling first impressions. Red flags and unrelenting depletion appear for a reason. You've made the correct move when your body stops fighting to wake and warn. From there, and when desperation isn't your tolerated state, progress follows.

Next, I'd tell her that the uncertainty accompanying change is not bad; it's a friend and an aspect of progression. Apprehension, and even fear, both indicate that the risk change asks you to take is important. Uncertainty means options and elbow room. Use it.

Those recurring thoughts about change dominate on purpose; earlier trust in my intuition could have avoided prolonging the unnecessary struggle.

You already know you have to make a move, so view change as an act of resisting whatever resistance looms, or a willingness to try something that's not guaranteed to work. Sometimes it doesn't. It's the long jump into an unknown sandpit with conviction that the sand's clean while the hand of reservation yanks at your ponytail. You must have a go to see.

Finally, my rundown would emphasise that life won't hurt anymore. Regret remains in the past, and the ability to give and receive more comes through healing, not holding on to suffering.

Thanks to these discoveries, none of which are universal truths, when change is next required, I'll remember it's not something to fear. It's a new opportunity or approach suited to the endeavour. And so, I will revisit the affirmation that change might be both the way and a chance to embrace self-leadership while braving full responsibility.

Boundaries as the outlines for life

T he pervasiveness of burnout implies I should do my part. Is there a way my experience could aid someone else's comeback? The answer's *yes*; to help another is a viable dream. I'd like to be an example, one of confidence in boundaries and change.

Of course, it's not as straightforward as compiling my journals in an attempt at a book. Self-help is *self* helping *self*. No one can do that for anyone else, but all that aids the reclaiming of limits, sanity and life holds power, if shared. I searched for help, for resonance in books, looking for relatable predicaments and reassurance. I wanted to relate to someone who'd made it through, to grasp prospect and proof of coming out alright post change. I collected knowledge and inspiration, but not a transferable story.

However, I experienced the gratification of reigniting my once-dwindling self, proving that turnarounds are real. They're not mythical at all. Turns out, I sought an account not yet shared— mine. And if there's potential to relay something beneficial, I want to do that.

I won't be able to cover it all, given the broad variables to burnout and healing too. Instead, my words inspect the havoc that ignoring burnout can cause, a bird's-eye view of a single journey, not advice or suggested to-dos. I hope to impart that self-help is *self*-help and that boundaries, as the outlines of a lovely existence, serve only if applied.

There's merit in hope, in stories inspiring us to have a go. Somehow, I implemented the changes required. If I hadn't located that resolve, I'm not sure where I'd be today. This is reason enough to spread any lived messages of hope.

Although hope's a peachy sentiment, burnout was not a nice ailment to disclose. Instinct said hold it close and reserve vulnerability for behind the facade. Perfectionism long reminded me that the ideal thing to do is to keep it together, with extra charm. That's when I lost. I had no choice. I had to change. Others would fold under such pressures, too.

It came as a surprise, but disclosure grants a gateway to a bright unknown. Once I raised my hand to admit my struggle, burnout switched costumes, becoming a new character, the impetus pointing me back towards life.

Burnout morphed into a reminder, a sign, revealing my unintended detour from a healthy path. I was the problem. I allowed demands to creep. My pastimes included people-pleasing and committing to the highest degree. I built a fabulous, secure cage. Isolated yet surrounded, longing for solitude. My fantasy was for everyone to leave me alone, if only for a minute. I gave up on sensible limits, and I did what I needed to do, exceeding each brief and attracting more work. Loaded with responsibility felt special. Last on my list, but talented at finding hours that didn't exist for any other list, I devalued my needs to the edge of extremes.

To overcome burnout, I had to flip things around and use my energy and drive towards healthier pursuits. Ways of coping, ways of doing, ways of living to recharge, not drain. I'm working at it, through the flat days and occasional ephemeral memories of old stress and past ways. I aspired to make it through a difficult time. Everything's a continuation of that. I'm now penning the book I needed, the example I searched for. It wasn't the plan, but there's been *aha* moments throughout and more upcoming, no doubt. The future looks grander each day.

To read my journals back is akin to me running my hand over a piece of handmade furniture that someone's gone to lengths to restore. The preserved yet imperfect woodgrain tells an authentic tale, despite the original item emerging renewed and ready for a new purpose. Sigh, is it a worry I referred to myself as a worn yet reborn piece of furniture? I say no. There's no need for concern if I'm rolling with the assortment of weirdness and beauty that healing brings, if I'm moving closer to contributing something to the many comrades in arms.

My part, I hope it's this…

To show it is possible to burn out but also enhance the qualities that are the prerequisites of success. To relay that contentment is within reach. For me, this morning, that looked like building Lego with the boys on the rug. And one day, to pass on two words: please try!

20 October 2024

Solutions from the soul

Under the sky-scraping trees, grass dewy and lush underhand, my calves are folded under my thighs, hips resting over heels, waiting for the next instruction. "Now, wrap your arms around yourself and hold for a few breaths." Despite coming from my phone, the yoga instructor's composed voice adds to the scene.

Inhale the freshness of the breeze combing through my hair and touching the soles of my feet.
Exhale, still hugging myself.
Inhale, exhale, yoga in the yard is so nice.
Inhale, dog licking my face. "Sit, Chase."

Exhale, get back to relaxed amongst the lively chorus of birds.

Inhale, exhale—what a release for my upper back.

Inhale, can the neighbours see me hugging myself in the garden like a nutcase?

Exhale, who cares?

Inhale, the blocks of land *will* sell soon, sustaining this way of life.

Exhale and stop fretting about it. Long-term financial stability is coming. In time.

Inhale self-forgiveness, knowing I won't repeat the mistakes around overwork and stress ever again.

Exhale all remaining regret about working to breaking point while calling it success.

I thought I'd forgiven everything I did to myself, but in my few mindful breaths today, a new finality joined me on the mat. I forgive myself for being complicit.

The solution existed within; I had to change to grow. I helped myself, and now I'm a more present parent. There's no impressive answer or excuse for why I deluded myself for so long, except to admit my once pleasant path lost connection with the sun. What I normalised was worlds away from right, and that's the madness in it all; that's burnout. I should have known better and changed earlier, but now, walking back up to the house after yoga, my angst about perpetuating burnout fades, my longest exhale ever. I prevailed.

23 October 2024

My thoughts on holding back

I magine the occasional sprinkle of pixie dust sufficing in real life to help us along, to assist with direction, to help us say yes. Sometimes it may, depending on my outlook and what I do next. Thoughts circle in relation to releasing or withholding my words, the ones I write here in my journal. It's a mix of *heck yes* and *oh my gosh, no.*

With motivations for and against, questions about overshare and self-indulgence surface again and again. Being self-absorbed helped me heal. But I suffered no trauma. Do I risk offending or upsetting anyone with my story? Burnout is on me; have I made that clear enough throughout? Is writing about myself the embodiment of vanity? There's also the daunting query of whether I'm fearless enough to be vulnerable, to let my guard down forever. That's what this is if I release it—an open viewing of my weaknesses and flaws. An unnerving call. Maybe no one will read it, and it will sit on my shelf; for me, that's a comforting notion.

But…

What if it didn't fail and instead contributed? This is possible too. This is the attitude needed to stifle the rest of these thoughts I'm working through today. Let's try that. Plus, finishing a book is the ultimate individual success. If I can do this, I'm testing and proving the theory of trusting myself. Combine this with my next pro-publishing argument and I'd be remiss to vote no. If the aim of change is to secure sustained freedom, is this a step towards that goal? How significant is this attempt to the entirety of life? My resistance is either the tip-off that my writing has the legs to mature or it's time to stop.

After all, the words dropped in my lap like rain from the clouds; getting them down on paper was effortless. I assume there's a reason for that flow. Could it be traces of that mystical pixie powder? Something glittery garnishes my creative process, rewarding me as I go. Either that, or my whimsical self-belief is part of this dreamy state. Time and trust will tell, but for now I'm talking/writing around my thoughts on holding back. Share away, go with that.

27 October 2024

All that sparkles

Spending a weekend afternoon helping Mike next door pack his life into boxes was a constructive way to end the day. We sorted a lifetime's worth of treasures into boxes labelled *keep, donate* and *discard*. Today was just one of a few packing sessions, because his home is as full as his life.

We love to chat while we pack. Mike's got plenty to say; his wisdom is as sharp as his wit and occasional risqué humour. A straight-talking type of guy who's seen and done it all; a genuine character. We'll miss him and will stay in touch.

My heart swelled with spaciousness when, between taping boxes, he offered me a collection of crystal glassware, vases and hand-painted fine bone china. The finest of flowers, captured in delicate brushstrokes, wrapped around the daintiest of gold-rimmed teacups. A trove I couldn't accumulate, let alone afford.

"Mike, which box for these?" I asked, gently lifting the delicate porcelain.

"Choose what you'd like. I want you to take some. I'll keep a bit too and donate the rest," he replied.

Unsure how to express the appropriate level of thanks, I found my words about eight seconds into my awkward silence. "Mike, what? Surely there's someone in your family you'd prefer to give these to."

"They're yours, girl," he said with a chuckle and exhale of smoke from his pipe while using his wheelie walker as a seat.

Treasuring the pieces is how I'll relay my gratitude. My initial hesitation mellowed into sincere appreciation. We'll think of Mike with each sip from the items passed on.

As we packed, it struck me that this accumulation of domestic treasure symbolises more than mere possessions. It's about memory, friendship, offerings and the sparkles of human connection. To make a slight difference to someone, to cook a few meals, fill a glass now and again and assemble some boxes—that's invaluable. I didn't comprehend that I deserved such kindness in return. There's much to cherish; the reminiscence this boon will long provide in respect and thanks to our friend Mike is one example.

Prior to heading home to get dinner on, while perfecting the sticky tape dispenser reload and assembling, stacking and securing cardboard boxes, I got it. My healing shares commonalities with packing and moving, and even refined crystal. Keep, value, uphold or abandon, reject, remove—all ongoing choices, in packing and in life. And like Mike's crystal, healing too holds the ability to refract some stunning light. Coincidental? Perhaps not. Thank you, Mike!

Late afternoon, 28 October 2024

Settling into calm

This morning's early walk in the drizzling rain is the refreshing shower that made my day. I'm living countless moments like this, where the ordinary becomes the incredible. On arrival home, with much to accomplish (the usual, one thing at a time, yay), the day kept providing. It appears heaven on earth is a hike in the rain to acknowledge my Monday at home basking in the silence, lapping up the focus and calm.

Despite the serenity, I owe a lot to my choices, sacrifices and the experience and opportunity attained through past work. Life's different now, but everything along the way played its part.

Mid-writing, I received a message from work, not asking me to do anything, not dragging me into the hollow of noise disguised as urgency, but to say hello and share some news. That's all. I was included and needed but not burdened to solve anyone's problem. It's noteworthy and complements my simplified wardrobe of rearranged priorities. These new relaxed indigo-wash jeans, they fit so well. The promised land does exist. My new part-time job has all the makings of ideal and encouraging. New skills procured and old ones applied, it will lead somewhere positive. It already has—I'm not infinitely rostered on!

With freedom in tow, I'm setting out on the next stage of whatever this time is, laying more yellow brick road track beyond joy's initial gate. Grounded, ready, certain, the surrounding energy sure beats a confirmatory pulse. There's stress that serves, motivates and prompts me for more. I enjoy this, no longer fragile and torn in five directions. Instead, I'm curious as the days flutter and fluctuate. I didn't conceive all of this as part of my world.

Evening of 28 October 2024

A baby bird they named Frederick the First

Nurturing is innate, the boys reminded me the other day. Jackson's face lit up as a wild baby bird flew out of the tree and onto my back while I was grabbing the dog leads from the boot. As if it wanted to say hello, the bird made the short flight over to Jackson's shoulder, then to Leo's. Interested in us, this noisy little leatherhead, still fluffy under the neck, wasn't afraid.

"Is he lost, Mum? How can we help him?" Jackson asked.

"He's tame, hey boys. Let's see what he needs. We can help him get back to his nest."

"Yes, and we should call him Frederick," Leo said without hesitation, even though *he* may have been a *she*.

Besotted and slipping into caring mode, the boys' voices were loving and their movements gentle as they spoke to the little bird, curious about their new friend. And friends they became for an afternoon. The bird didn't want to leave their shoulders; he wanted in, to be part of the cul-de-sac kid crew. As they enjoyed another outdoor adventure caring for the bird, this memory in the making developed a power to give on repeat.

The bird wouldn't go, despite having already mastered flight. It wasn't interested in returning to the tree, either. The boys rallied neighbours, parading down the tranquil street, bird on arm, head and handlebars. "Hey, look at this baby bird. We're helping him. His name is Frederick."

They smiled and giggled, captivated as the bird devoured the deep-lavender mulberries they picked from the backyard tree. "Have this berry. It's a ripe one." Next, they pinched tiny pieces of mince. Our two rough-and-tumble boys, embracing their roles as tender caregivers, sustained the bird with company, food, water and little-boy love.

Before bed, they set up an expansive open-door aviary in the entrance area near the tree and kept ducking out to check. "Are you okay, buddy?" they'd ask. Frederick rested until dawn and squawked some more prior to taking flight back to nature, ahead of the kids waking for the day. Their job—nurturing a free but friendly and hungry bird—was done. Both bird and boys received more than adventure and a refuel. Wherever Frederick's now perched, we hope he (or she) also gained from the encounter.

The point is, I was home, around to take part. We all grew this week. Frederick flew into our lives to hang out for the afternoon, free, yet eager to be with us.

"I hope Freddy visits again," Leo told me. "It's okay either way, Mum, because from now on, each bird that gets close, we will name Frederick the Second, or Frederick Two, Three, Four, or however many more."

When Leo was small, he'd say, right after an embrace or doing something beyond cute (and he was tight-ringlet curls, bronzed and delicious kind of cute), "Did that melt your heart, Mummy?" He doesn't ask anymore, but this week, both of my babies did just that. Thank you, burnout, for giving these dear parts of my life back.

29 October 2024

On top of our mountain, where it's
wildly beautiful

U p the mountain today, alone, to check it all. These trips
to the farm stir wonderment and daunting accountability.
It's difficult to explain the complexity of the emotion.
How does one quantify the breadth of nature untamed?

I'm pulled to go, that's all I know. Self-importance waits, hung
over the splintering post of the old rusty gate at the bottom of the
climb, ready for pick-up on my walk back down. I'll grab it before
returning home. The more time I spend here, paying attention or
making a pin drop of difference tending to the land, the more I
understand. I comprehend myself, Rob's adoration for his mountain
and its significance in my life. Sometimes I almost expect to see

him riding down to the gate, bareback on his horse to greet us, like he did when we were kids.

Sounds buzz electric and green and lilac carpets line the winding tracks; the wide alleyways of jacarandas are in full flower, a sight of mauve to behold. Spring flowers bloom too—tiny, pretty and poking through.

The grass is also once again elevated, the product of recent rains. In a simplistic sense, personal growth goes much the same way. Higher, lusher, measurable and visible development where watered, vivid in various shades, signalling all is well, progressing. There's not much further into nature or healing I could go.

I'll go as far as declaring that this mountain's alive. Butterflies galore, and some snakeskins as well. Rob's around, with nature resting beneath his tree, supervising progress incognito, as discreet as the native bees. He's grinning at our efforts and awakenings so far, despite dozer-loads for the rest of our lives more to do. Softly does it is the way to go; overwhelm prevails otherwise.

In maintaining the farm, we learn as we move through. The lesson is comprehending that the inputs required will have no end. The array of interconnected parts is not unlike the elaborate yet integral minutiae that comprise and sustain a well-lived life. Traction and harmony result if efforts repeat, at the farm and within. If only that prehistoric dozer rusting out on the property still ran!

There's something inspiring about the isolation here. It's full immersion. The expanse is intimidating, captivating, majestic, all at once. Looking down the valley offers a perspective that I'm small, another slight wildflower shouldering the grass. The farm's a zoom-out and zoom-in experience, and both lenses serve. But that's the point of mountains; they are vantage points that offer a view. Enhanced eyeshot and visibility of the contrasts, the bigger picture that encompasses the intertwined happenings below. They also ascend us closer to the sky. I'm closer to the upper atmosphere more often here, which could explain my recent spiritual finds.

Humans and mountains alike are ecosystems: surviving, regenerating and advancing in their own right. This is what I'm experiencing since burning out. Cycles. Butterflies of all sizes hover around—black, orange and muted colours too. Time stands still in my open-air conservatory, even on the walk back down.

Write, recover, edit, but do not perfect

The confusion in my sustained burnout state was immense, disorientating, crushing. So much so that I thought my two choices included giving up on life or the ruthless management on-call button, regardless of what I'd already accomplished or done. Thanks to a force that I can't put my finger on, I avoided the unthinkable and went on responding to the unending calls to assist. I deluded myself into thinking it was simply hard work.

No part of the above is easy to confess, but it's an example of what perfectionism looks like when it goes wrong. Sometimes, my attempts to better everything left me in pieces.

I spent my years optimising, perfecting, making things palatable and immaculate, with little regard for the toll. It's key to much of my success, but it also burnt me out. Therefore, in the spirit of change, I'll resist the impulse to perfect. In this new life, perfect dilutes the verity, emotion and impact of my story. Perfect is insipid; it wasn't real. I don't aspire to that. I'd rather be me. And if I'm going to share something, it may as well honour my truths. I won't edit to perfect or to protect my vulnerabilities. Instead, I'll revise in a way that promotes further expansion via reflection.

I'm nervous about revisiting May and June, those heavy, tear-filled months when I lived to serve and refine. What a waste of time.

Time and writing—that's what change gave me. Time to recover and uncover. Unpredicted, immediate and unexplainable levels of peace came first, followed by expected and ongoing flickers of hesitancy. Am I still working and delivering to my potential? Past me would say no, but considering my passion for my new situation and openness to achieving in different ways, today, *close enough* is nicer than an absolute, perfected *yes*. By no longer editing my life with earnest determination to be the best for everyone else, I earned this result.

3 November 2024

Bringing life back to life

Stay, inhale, appreciate and celebrate. It's all worthy of celebration; any journey is. Most end, and some continue. Mine will be lifelong.

Along the way, each tweak accumulates into a building confidence. I know how and when to walk away from conflict—internal, real or imagined. Fulfilled, living as I please, answering to high standards of a different sort. I didn't stumble onto this path. Pain shoved me onto it, depleted, in need of help. I faced it, examining the shattered actuality I called a life.

In waking up, I crawled forward until I could stride again. I rested, questioned and opened my heart and adored that part. A willingness to credit guidance from things larger than myself became my kind of bible. The pure-grade pages are velvety under my hand, almost affectionate.

From there, my world delivered for me as I delivered for it in the past, with open and kind counsel. There's no secret; I did the work. But this time it was distinct. It mattered. I met burnout for excellent reasons. For freedom, opportunity and growth. I also experienced firsthand that tables turn, minds change, and healing was not only achievable, but on standby. Light can follow dark. In my case, the darkness preceded a radiance, an unexplainable lustre. Likewise, my burnout experience teaches me that discomfort presents, niggles, and hurts *for* me. And this next declaration—the one where I claim the key traits that contributed to my downfall also enhanced my recovery—astounds, many times over. Post-burnout, the impossible became possible. Determination, diligence and discipline—they're the tools, and my commitment to quality, my sensitivity and tendency to over-deliver heal as much as they harmed.

As a result, I'll no longer underestimate the ability and opportunity to divert energy, to transfer perceived flaws or dire situations into life's greatest hits and leaps. Whatever the future holds, I have a fair idea of how it will feel, all threats removed. On that day in May, as I reached the apex of the unpleasant, I had to choose. I picked life dedicated to a different focus. I changed, and I'm moseying on in my unfolding, I'm eclipsing alright. The space where life comes back to life is where the butterflies reside. Now I do too.

10 November 2024

Promises to self

P romises to self—they're the arteries to the heart, oxygen to the brain, and at a basic, stripped-back level, they're all I have.

My vow to my past self
I'll hold in high regard the achievements and fundamentals I mastered, the shaping that occurred and the struggles I endured. I promise to be proud. Proud I did the tough years with grace and professionalism, for making a difference, despite winding up a little lost.

Pledge to my present self

I'm whole-body happy and promise to keep noticing that. I'll value these years. With the freedom and strength available, I will stay prepared to question and pivot, to view change as an opportunity. This means acknowledging real or perceived losses as mere trade-offs and not worrying about them too much. Nothing's out of reach, not the sublime dreams or maverick ideas. With this in mind, I promise to pursue meaningful outcomes, authentic emotion and the priorities that are mine.

Oath to my future self

I will be the old lady with the waist-long hair, surrounded by my family, books and all I adore. Home is here by the forest forever, enjoying the days, just being. I promise to be namaste-palms-pressed grateful for the things that pass me by, and to trust that what's correct will appear, stay and sustain. My oath is to do my best, but also to rest sometimes.

To all my selves, past, present and future, I promise to value the lessons of each woman, to rely on my intuition. You have my word.

Well and available

"How are you going?" asked my doctor during today's phone consultation.

"I'm really well, thank you." My immediate and unplanned response was honest, real, soul-filling. I blurted it out like an exuberant kid because, for the first time in years, it's true.

To say it without faking it, to mean it, marks progress in five short words. As I spoke into the phone, my wide smile illuminated the genuine landmark within. I stood taller, surer and lighter as my beaming enthusiasm highlighted how my situation's transformed. I witnessed it. The handset did too. The dining room also listened in. As for my doctor, he no doubt assumed I'd had too much coffee as we bounced through the pleasantries. But the cheer was all me.

It's a big moment: my default response with no prior thought was that I'm great, because I am.

I now enjoy freedoms, such as making plans for holidays and fun without worrying about what will pull me away, whether I will have to shorten the duration or if I'll even make it. I get to go, no elaborate fuss, just grab a ticket and sort the pups. To talk about things we'd like to experience minus the dread of how I'll be everywhere all at once is a passport to joy. My options are open; *choice* is my first-ever religion.

We may not venture far thanks to the homebody within, but that's beside the point. What counts is that my priorities have shifted, and in every way, I'm available. Excitement's building, and freedom pings intriguing—an undiscovered trail, a different mountain.

Actual trips aside, the anticipation and realisation of this availability and what it represents qualify as an appealing destination.

24 November 2024

Paying tribute to each day

Life's slower, but so full. Family dinners, late afternoon cook-ups and sunset refreshments with garnishes from the herb pot. This stage, this instalment, is about paying tribute to each day, not wishing them away. It's more than enough, this existence I now lead.

There are examples every day. Today, I worked for hours in the sun, push-mowing the back lawn, my excuse to be in the garden. It's medicinal, the highs of exertion and hot, sweaty bliss in our garden of Eden. Unlimited benefits despite the heat exposure. Opulence is having the time, and being healthy and able, to complete the task. Again, thank you, burnout.

Right on cue, an array of petite, daffodil-yellow and cotton-ball-white butterflies hovered in the yard to watch me perspire. They're regularly there, close to my face, so near I stop to say hello. They move together, up, up and around, creating smears of sugary buttercream across the backdrop of blue skies.

Too, the aromatics of the soil intensified the fresh potency of the grass clippings as I spread them. The angelic shower of colourful leaves, floating and descending, the insects going about their day alongside me, moving through mine. And so it goes, one action, one section of lawn after the last. It's how to mow and how I now roll. Burnout and I uncovered a depth of personality, exposing bona fide appreciation for the silver linings popping up daily.

Days like this remind me why I required a full revolution and evolution of both situation and self. They give back. My goal is more of the same. These plentiful lulls are not a pause before any crisis I need to manage. This is my everyday. I've got a few weeks' work to go ahead of holidays at home. A new concept, this chance to embrace life's new vibe, balmy and smelling of festive spice, sunscreen and iced sangria punch.

Truth is, it's not that I failed to cope. In my role of many things to many people, I delivered. But while testing limits and theories, I was careless personally, and burnout was the cost. However, burnout is both my black and my white swan, the experience directing me towards this superconscious beyond the void. It's possible the message in the wind, sky or the trees isn't about fighting for a fairy tale. Maybe it's about being receptive to finding the fairy tale in the most unexpected places because, thanks to burnout, I'm at home with my boys.

Epilogue

This memoir serves as another beginning, one that builds on the last.

It's March 2025 as I complete the last pages of the project that handed me back my life. As we brace for Cyclone Alfred on this eerie and uncertain Thursday afternoon, I'm not ensuring cold-chain storage viability or enacting a facility's emergency plan. I'm where I belong: at home, preparing for whatever's coming our way. We have the important things tied down, in order, and secured against any superstorm in more ways than one.

Leo's a week shy of ten, and Jackson will soon turn twelve. I'm the mum who picks them up from school a few days a week, attends footy training without my laptop and shares evening meals. We enjoy quiet, playful weekends and neighbourhood adventures. Sometimes all that means is hanging out together in the backyard, a jump on the trampoline (the kelpies first on), handball on the driveway or netting a few hoops at the end of the cul-de-sac at sunset. I also mastered the art of losing at chess to preteens. Leo, while gloating well before each cheeky victory, somehow manoeuvres both sets of kings and queens. The boys are protective, adamant that it's better to have me around. "I like having you here more," they tell me. "Don't be gone like before."

In keeping with my commitment to the boys, while enjoying the achievements of work, I continue in my part-time role in medical administration for an inspiring women's health specialist. Boundaries exist, and there's a happiness in the unlikely alignment of it all. This deliberate reduction is a step up into something exceptional. A level up in life. Work is work, home is home. This book wouldn't have happened had I launched myself back into the enormity of Burnout Incorporated. I wouldn't have this life, one where I write daily in the spare moments between the kids, work and maintaining the mountain as a family.

The farm is an evolving legacy of education, responsibility and joy. Between the creek and the farm, those little flutters of knowing are ever abundant. These days, I observe signs of life and live by the philosophies that came to my aid.

Hence, my circle's small, my home is my haven and I'm careful about how I spend my time. I'm intentional in my preference for a simpler life. Introversion, nature, minimalism and simplicity are life support to the burnt out and the actual heroes of this story. They helped me see that purpose existed within all along. Passive and patient, but powerful, leaving clues, tracks to follow on the path. They waited for me to race around the gameboard a few more times, appearing with force when I next approached *Go* and adjusting the board to read *Stop*.

For this reason and others, burnout, in my book, was my ultimate formative experience. The why was as important to explore as the what-comes-next. Methods of recovery emerge with each sunrise, but it's our choice how we use and traverse the day.

Hello life of sunshine, a different calibre of shiny. The becoming where kindness is not a weakness, where I'm land-, life- and asset-rich, a tad cash-strapped at times (the block sales will settle soon), but completely assured. I've made it to the end of all my rainbows. Thank you, burnout.

Acknowledgements

I feel immense gratitude and owe many thanks.

Showered with support, a magnificent childhood, love, mentors and opportunities galore, my difficulties are minuscule compared to the trauma out there.

Life gifts particular experiences and people into our orbit, and I'm blessed with those in mine.

Jackson and Leo, you are my greatest loves and the best little dudes. You are my reason for change, why I had to do better. Being your mum is the priority, and I will marvel as you grow for the rest of my days.

Steven, I love you. Together we've faced highs, disappointments and many wins. We've built a life based on honesty and integrity, and this makes me happy. You're a man who sets the example. You also challenge me often, which keeps things interesting. Thank you for all you do and for not judging me as I sat many afternoons converting my journals in the garden.

And speaking of unwavering support, there are no words grand enough or pages spacious enough to express the love and gratitude I hold for my parents, Suzette and Steve. You gave me everything, listened and backed me. You are the angels everyone wishes for. Thanks, Mum and Dad, I love you.

The family support, love and thanks extend to my brother Matthew and sister-in-law Brie. Matty, I treasure all we share, our chats and farm working bees. Brie, you predicted and prompted a nicer way forward before I was aware I had a choice. Thank you.

It makes sense that the only centenarian I'm fortunate to know and love (so far) had the answers. Grandma Betty, your wisdom, your welcome, your love of nature and simplicity live on. I hope to be like you—at home, self-sufficient, humble and at peace in my own company. Thank you for the life example.

To my closest friends in no set order—Eva, April, Kim and Negra, you are wonderful in every way. Thank you for listening and encouraging. Conversations shared over prosecco and cheap Thai dinners sustained me. You assured me that choosing my needs is more than okay. I hope I'm there to rally for you. Guess what? The neurosurgeon we share consulting rooms with described me as *calming*. True story.

Thank you to my remarkable mentors, colleagues and family members for entrusting me with important responsibilities, projects to manage and problems to solve. You helped me grow. I also owe gratitude to anyone I've ever let down. To the team I adored but had to hand over during difficult times. To my family, who watched me choose my job over what matters. Thank you for your understanding. You were all so kind.

I extend a huge thank you to the inspiring Jessica Mudditt and her impressive publishing team at Hembury Books. Thanks to you, my book now sits on my bookshelf. You made my story tangible.

Overall, I'm grateful for my burnout experience and the intuition that guided me through. Burnout was the crossroads where I found the answers to my life. My faith in something larger continues to expand. From depletion to peace, I'm fortunate I landed here, in a far better place than where I began.

www.ingramcontent.com/pod-product-compliance
Lightning Source LLC
Chambersburg PA
CBHW032003050726
47590CB00006B/2027

MINISTÈRE DE LA GUERRE

—

DÉCRET DU 26 OCTOBRE 1883

PORTANT RÈGLEMENT SUR LE

SERVICE DES ARMÉES

EN CAMPAGNE

PARIS

LIBRAIRIE MILITAIRE DE BERGER-LEVRAULT ET Cⁱᵉ

Éditeurs de l'Annuaire de l'Armée

5, RUE DES BEAUX-ARTS, 5

Même maison à Nancy

DÉCRET DU 26 OCTOBRE 1883

PORTANT RÈGLEMENT SUR LE

SERVICE DES ARMÉES

EN CAMPAGNE

NANCY, IMP. BERGER-LEVRAULT ET Cie.